Scenarios in Public Policy

Scenarios in Public Policy

Gill Ringland

JOHN WILEY & SONS LTD

Other Wiley Editorial Offices

John Wiley & Sons, Inc., 605 Third Avenue,
New York, NY 10158-0012, USA

Wiley-VCH Verlag GmbH, Pappelallee 3,
D-69469 Weinheim, Germany

John Wiley & Sons Australia Ltd., 33 Park Road, Milton,
Queensland 4064, Australia

John Wiley & Sons (Asia) Pte Ltd, 2 Clementi Loop #02-01,
Jin Xing Distripark, Singapore 129809

John Wiley & Sons (Canada) Ltd, 22 Worcester Road,
Rexdale, Ontario M9W 1L1, Canada

British Library Cataloguing in Publication Data
A catalogue record for this book is available from the British Library

ISBN 0-470-84383-7

Project management by Originator, Gt Yarmouth (typeset in 11/13pt Garamond)
Printed and bound in Great Britain by T.J. International Ltd, Padstow, Cornwall
This book is printed on acid-free paper responsibly manufactured from sustainable forestry,
in which at least two trees are planted for each one used for paper production.

Contents

About the author   vii

Acknowledgements   ix

Abbreviations   xi

Introduction   1

Part I **SCENARIOS IN PUBLIC POLICY**   7
          Summary   7
          I.1   Four scenarios for public education in Seattle   11
          I.2   Rotterdam and Arnhem   20
          I.3   Mission and consequences in Bueren   23
          I.4   Scottish Enterprise's use of scenarios   31
          I.5   Tackling big issues in 24 hours   42
          I.6   Scenarios for sustainable development   51
          I.7   VISIONS scenarios on the future of Europe   57
          I.8   Foresight Futures 2001   65
          I.9   Lessons learned   77

Part II **SCENARIOS IN THE PUBLIC SECTOR**   81
           Summary   81
           II.1   US General Services Agency – scenarios for   83
                  the federal workplace
           II.2   Consignia and scenario thinking   94
           II.3   Scenarios at the dti   104
           II.4   Scenario planning goes to Rome   111
           II.5   Decision making in the public sector   124
           II.6   Lessons learned   132

Part III **MAKING SCENARIOS WORK**   135
    Summary   135
    III.1 The environment for scenario thinking   137
    III.2 The stages of a project   145
    III.3 Getting started   153
    III.4 Deciding the question   160
    III.5 Interviews and workshops   167
    III.6 Scenario creation   176
    III.7 Scenarios to plans   185
    III.8 Linking scenarios into the organization   194
    III.9 Main points   200

Part IV **SCENARIO THINKING**   203
    Summary   203
    IV.1 Scenarios and strategy   205
    IV.2 Strategy and scenario planning in the   211
          public sector
    IV.3 Where are we now?   217
    IV.4 Forecasts   223
    IV.5 Evolutionary models for cultural change   230
    IV.6 Comparison of global scenarios   242
    IV.7 Where next?   250
    IV.8 Conclusions   255

References   257

Index   263

About the author

Gill Ringland graduated as a physicist, spending two years at the University of California at Berkeley and a year as a Fellow at Oxford. After working for an expanding computer software house, a start-up, and a US company, Gill built a number of businesses inside ICL before becoming Group Executive responsible for strategy. She then started The Lifestyle Network – to study the changes in consumer lifestyles, now adopted by the Cranfield School of Management as part of their New Marketing Research Club. She has worked with a number of organizations on strategic issues, focusing on future-resilient decision making.

She is a Liveryman of the City of London, a Fellow of the BCS, a Member of the IEEE, a past Member of the Computing Science Committee of the UK's Science Research Council and a Council Member of the Economic and Social Research Council, an ICL Fellow Emeritus, and author of *Scenario Planning – Managing for the Future*, also published by John Wiley & Sons, Ltd. She is a Fellow of St Andrews Management Institute and can be contacted on gill.ringland@btinternet.com.

Acknowledgements

As the century turned and the pace of life grew ever more frenetic, the question was asked: Is there a need for "The Art of the Short View"? – referring to Peter Schwartz's classic book on scenarios, *The Art of the Long View* (Schwartz, 1997). This book brings together thinking about the future and recognizing models of the world, and ways of making better decisions in business in the short as well as the long term.

It is the result of many conversations and shared experiences with people concerned to improve business effectiveness. It tries to address the questions most frequently asked, as well as those that should be asked, by people concerned to discover whether they should use scenarios in their organizations, as well as those wanting to use them more effectively.

It is the product of a virtual team of thinkers and practitioners: Frans Berkhout, Clem Bezold, Adrian Blumfield, George Burt, Napier Collyns, Adrian Davies, Ged Davis, Chris Ertel, Alexander Fink, Maureen Gardiner, Philip Hadridge, Barbara Heinzen, Julia Hertin, Glen Hiemstra, Tony Hodgson, Annette Hutchinson, Eamonn Kelly, Jaap Leemhuis, Tom Ling, Peter McKiernan, Nancy Murphy, Richard O'Brien, Jay Ogilvy, Drew Overpeck, John Reynolds, Sue Roberts, Jan Rotmans, Gareth Price, Kent Potter, Peter Schwartz, Adam Scott, Oliver Sparrow, Jonathan Star, Rohit Talwar, Philip van Notten, George Vervuurt and many others. To all, my sincere thanks for their ideas, their thinking and their vision; and to those, in addition, who contributed sections or case studies, my debt is clearly visible and acknowledged with their contributions.

Additionally, my thanks are due to Napier Collyns and Sue Roberts for reading the manuscript and providing suggestions that have immeasurably improved the book.

And, not least, my heartfelt thanks to Gordon Ringland who added insight at points where it was needed, and to Diane Taylor of John Wiley who published the first "Scenario Planning" book and encouraged this and its sister book to follow it up.

Parts of this book are based on case studies or discussion from *Scenario Planning – Managing for the Future* and these are reproduced by permission of John Wiley & Sons, Ltd.

Abbreviations

B2B	Business-to-Business
BCS	British Computer Society
BSE	Bovine Spongiform Encephalopathy
CSERGE	Centre for Social and Economic Research on the Global Environment
dti	UK Department of Trade and Industry
ECU	European Currency Unit
ESRC	Economic and Social Research Council
EU	European Union
FF	Faster, Faster
FROG	First Raise Our Growth
FUD	Fear, Uncertainty and Doubt
GBN	Global Business Network
GMO	Genetically Modified Organism
GSA	General Services Agency
IAF	Institute for Alternative Futures
ICAEW	Institute of Chartered Accountants in England and Wales
ICIS	International Centre for Integrative Studies
ICL	ICL, previously International Computers Ltd
ICT	Information and Communication Technologies
IDON	IDON Group, now called Metabridge
IEEE	Institute of Electrical and Electronic Engineers
IPCC	Intergovernmental Panel on Climate Change
IW	Industrialized World
JAZZ	Scenario in which developments are ad hoc
NIC	Newly Industrialized Countries
NGO	Non-Governmental Organization
NUD*IST	A software product

NWDMC	National Water Demand Management Centre
PEST	Political, Economic, Social, Technological
PIMS	Performance Impact of Market Strategy
PIR	Post-Industrial Revolution
PIU	Performance and Innovation Unit
REGIS	REGional Climate Change Impact and response Studies in East Anglia and North West England
RN	Rough Neighbours
S4S	Scenarios for Scotland
ScMI	Scenario Management International AG
SE	Scottish Enterprise
SF	Scotland's Future
SFT	Strategic Futures Team
SGI	Silicon Graphics
SME	Small and Medium-sized Enterprise
SPRU	Science and Technology Policy Research, University of Sussex
SRES	Special Report on Emissions Scenarios
SRI	Stanford Research Institute
SWOT	Strength, Weakness, Opportunities, Threats
TPG	The holding company of Nederlands Royal PTT Post and TNT
VTOL	Vertical Take Off and Landing (aircraft)
WBCSD	World Business Countil for Sustainable Development
WIRED	A magazine

INTRODUCTION

THE AUDIENCE FOR THIS BOOK

This book focuses on the use of scenarios for developing public policy. It covers both the use of scenarios to engage external stakeholders in decision making and their use internally within the public sector. It is intended for practising managers who would like to bring scenarios into their organization, or have experience of scenarios but would like to ensure that they know of best practice elsewhere. It is also designed to be useable on Management courses, as it is built of biteable chunks that can be read independently of the published order to meet specific needs.

There is a parallel book to this that focuses on the use of scenarios in the private sector, *Scenarios in Business*. While the use of scenarios started in the 1960s in public policy debates, much of the publicized use more recently has been in business. However, recently, interest in scenarios in the public sector has increased. Two themes emerge: the similarity of much usage in the public sector to that in business, for exploring changes in the external environment, and the usage for creating a shared vision among stakeholders – voters and citizens – to steer future developments. Both of these have strong echoes in the directions that scenario thinking is taking in the private sector.

THE CHALLENGE

There has been much discussion at the dawn of the new century about *the* many challenges faced by society. Despite dazzling technological progress, many of our social structures have not matched the pace of change; for example, biotechnology and information technology issues remain poorly integrated into our ethical, social or legal framework.

The new global politics, driven by instant TV coverage and the empowerment of people, focuses on wants rather than needs and is different from the world known for much of the last century. Also, concerns grow about our ability to maintain our physical environment.

This world is more complex than that envisaged when many of our institutions were created, and the institutions are now creaking, facing significant new challenges and pressures. It is tough to be a manager in a time of such uncertainty. Decisions taken today will have effects years hence – but in what sort of world? Futurists have conflicting views on the extent and nature of differences and similarities between today and the future. This situation is further complicated by confusion about the present, the fact that more than ever "today" is far from static: it is harder than ever to discern current trends and realities. At a time when the pace of change requires managers to make decisions at more junior levels than before, it is increasingly difficult to make well-informed decisions. There are no silver bullets.

WHAT ARE SCENARIOS?

The word "scenario" is used in many ways. Military scenarios are detailed contingency plans for a wide range of eventualities; in the creative media, it may mean a storyline; financial controllers use the term to mean sensitivity analysis; and strategists, policy makers and planners use scenarios in a "future-oriented" sense – and it is this that is the focus of this book.

Michael Porter defined scenarios as used in strategy (Porter, 1985) as:

> ... *An internally consistent view of what the future might turn out to be – not a forecast, but one possible future outcome.*

Scenarios are possible views of the world, providing a context in which managers can make decisions. By seeing a range of possible worlds, decisions will be better informed and a strategy based on this knowledge and insight will be more likely to succeed. Scenarios may not predict the future, but they do illuminate the drivers of change – understanding these can only help managers to take greater control of their situation. In this book, the case studies include the use of scenarios in the public sector to:

- imagine new consumers and new political environments;

- to deal with the new challenges, such as e-commerce and e-government; and

- to encourage participation and debate about the future in countries, cities and regions.

Additionally, scenario thinking is increasingly being used as a way of creating a shared view among a management team. Scenario thinking, by setting discussions in a time frame beyond their current assignment and beyond facts and forecasts, allows for a discussion with less defensive behaviour and a more shared sense of purpose.

SCENARIOS AND MANAGEMENT TECHNIQUES

Managers already have access to a number of strategic management toolkits that can improve the quality of decisions. This book provides the background and case studies to allow managers to place scenarios alongside these tools. Scenarios provide additional tools for managers to tackle these complexities, enabling better decision making, especially during times of uncertainty and risk. Scenarios are often used alongside standard techniques, although there is an important distinction. Scenarios are tools for examining possible futures. This gives them a clear and distinctive role compared with most toolkits or techniques that are based on a view of the past. In a rapidly changing and largely unpredictable environment, assessing possible futures is one of the best ways to promote responsiveness and directed policy. Understanding and preparing for the future is certainly possible through scenario planning.

This book is designed for managers who recognize the complexities of managing in a world where the only constant is change, and, increasingly, the only certainty is uncertainty.

THE BENEFITS OF THE SCENARIO APPROACH

Scenarios have been in use at Royal Dutch Shell since the 1960s, largely driven by one of the founders of modern scenario thinking in business, Pierre Wack. The main benefits of scenarios are outlined by Shell[1]:

Scenarios help us to understand today better by imagining tomorrow, increasing the breadth of vision and enabling us to spot change earlier.

Effective future thinking brings a reduction in the level of "crisis management" and improves management capability, particularly change management.

Scenarios provide an effective mechanism for assessing existing strategies and plans and developing and assessing options.

Royal Dutch Shell also point out the benefits of participating in a scenario building process:

Participating in the scenario building process improves a management team's ability to manage uncertainty and risk. Risky decisions become more transparent and key threats and opportunities are identified.

The participatory and creative process sensitizes managers to

---

[1]For further information see 'Scenarios – an Introduction', on www.shell.com

the outside world. It helps individuals and teams learn to recognize the uncertainties in their operating environments, so that they can question their everyday assumptions, adjust their mental maps, and truly think "outside the box" in a cohesive fashion.

HOW THIS BOOK IS ORGANIZED

This book is divided into four parts. *Part I* contains case studies to illustrate the scope and range of successful scenario usage in encouraging participative dialogue in relation to public policy on governmental or environmental issues. *Part II* describes projects to use scenarios within the public sector, whether to develop new strategy or to examine options. As acknowledged individually, many of the case studies have been contributed by the manager or team leader responsible.

Part III is concerned with 'Making scenarios work' and provides a collection of action-oriented checklists. They aim to act as a reminder rather than a first introduction, and are based on personal experience. *Part IV* describes the framework for scenario thinking, its history, the problems in forecasting, and where we are now – why organizations use scenario planning and in what circumstances. It also introduces two global scenarios.

In this Introduction and in Part IV some paragraphs are printed in bold italic: these are sections which are particularly useful for those trying to grasp the reasons for the successes of scenarios thinking in the organizations that have used them.

HOW SCENARIO THINKING IS CHANGING

This book builds on *Scenario Planning – Managing for the Future*, which was published in 1997. That book reflected what I found out as I used scenarios as a practising manager up to 1996, and contained much source material on methodologies, scenarios and case studies.

Some things have not changed since then – venture capitalists still bemoan the "one world" vision of business plans, major corporations are taken by surprise by changes in customer behaviour, new opportunities and new competition, and countries are taken by surprise by new challenges from inside and outside their borders. But, since 1997, scenario thinking has moved further into the mainstream for strategy and planning. And scenarios are increasingly being used as tools for knowledge management of complex worlds and as management development tools.

The applications of scenarios have changed their emphasis: in 1997, scenarios were often aligned with corporate planning and portfolio management. Now, scenarios are well established in the public sector. Here, they are as often concerned with dealing with new structural challenges as in getting the big picture right. One of the exciting growing uses of scenarios is for public policy, to create a common language and vision in a city, country or on environmental issues, as in the case studies in Part I.

In the public sector, the case studies of the US General Services Agency dealing with a new role, Consignia personalizing customers of the future to develop new markets, or Christian Brothers anticipating the next century, all demonstrate public sector or voluntary organizations using scenarios in a similar way to private-sector organizations.

This book reflects the world of the new century, the new environment for strategy and for scenarios – and tries to anticipate those further changes yet to come.

PART I
SCENARIOS IN PUBLIC POLICY

SUMMARY

This part contains descriptions of scenarios projects that have been designed to expose choices and provide a framework for debate about the future within the relevant constituency – whether a city or region, or large corporations and governments.

SCENARIOS FOR CITIES AND REGIONS

In each of these case studies, common factors were the wide involvement of citizens and elected officials in both the creation of the scenarios and in implementation of the choices.

In Seattle, the school system was underfunded and the staff demoralized, with a flight to the suburbs. After the scenarios project, school bonds were raised and a number of innovations on use of IT in schools and use of schools by the community were successful and being emulated elsewhere.

In Holland, Rotterdam celebrated 50 years of post-war rebuilding and looked ahead to 2045: Where should the new Rotterdam port be sited? Town meetings and then walkthrough scenarios encouraged public debate in Rotterdam, and then the planners of Arnhem to adopt the idea. In Arnhem, a Villa 2015 was created for each of the four scenarios and visitors were asked to vote on their favourite future.

Bueren in Germany used scenarios to develop missions and consequences or initiatives, which were then promoted by named prominent local individuals, and created a range of new voluntary groupings to tackle problems.

SCENARIOS FOR COUNTRIES

Scenarios used as metaphors to explore the choices facing a country are very powerful. The examples of South Africa (Kahane, 1997) and Canada, (Rosell (ed.), 1995) had a wide impact. The case study on Scotland by Scottish Enterprise brings out lessons about consultation, creation of vision and methods for communication. The example of short workshops to focus on specific issues – such as the Information Society in Europe – shows their use in bridging cultural divides.

SCENARIOS FOR THE ENVIRONMENT

Three very different uses of scenarios for the environment are described. The World Business Council on Sustainability is focused on the role of corporates, and the scenarios developed by them have been used by member companies and in discussions with national governments.

The VISIONS project developed integrated visions of Europe in 2050, based on work with over 200 people and groups, with ages ranging from school age to 60+. The scenarios relate to environmental aspects such as transport, water, energy and infrastructure and are available on a website and CD-ROM to support other groups using the models.

The Foresight scenarios in the UK were originally developed to describe environmental challenges but have been extended and used by a wide range of government departments and agencies to stimulate their thinking about the future in a number of workshops and projects.

LESSONS LEARNED

There are many similarities in the case studies reflected in the lessons learned:

- the importance of getting the context right;

- the ability of scenarios to simplify complexity and so help to galvanize community involvement;

- the use of scenarios to support further investigation into more detail, or into shocks to the system.

Four scenarios for public education in Seattle

This case study summarizes an innovative approach to strategic planning undertaken by the teachers' union, the Seattle Education Association, with the aid of Global Business Network, a research and consulting company specializing in the development of alternative scenarios for strategic planning. It describes scenarios for the future of education and how they have been used in Seattle: it is published by permission of the authors Roger Erskine and Jay Ogilvy.

BACKGROUND

Before the scenario project, Seattle's public schools were something of an embarrassment. With white flight to the suburbs, Seattle got hollowed out. Between 1980 and 1990, enrolment in Seattle's public schools dropped more than 10 per cent. The voters turned against the schools. School bond issues failed in every election from 1992 to 1996. And, of course, the teachers' union looked the worse for "the decline in public education".

THE SCENARIO PROJECT

The Seattle scenarios project included representatives of many different constituencies on the scenario team. The scenario process itself was part of the process of reform. By joining the representative constituents of the public education system together as a scenario planning team, the project process began to implement one of its eventual strategic options, namely:

Create a team with as much diversity as possible: old/young, male/female, senior/junior, white/black, different constituencies in the public for public schools, from the largest employer in Seattle, Boeing, to someone from City Hall, a successful business-man on the school board, several union leaders, an economist, and ten more selected for the range of their representation.

In order to arrive at a set of scenarios that highlight the critical uncertainties in Seattle's future, the scenario team developed a long list of relevant issues, then prioritized and aggregated some short lists to identify driving trends.

Discussion of the top-scoring items, together with closely related issues, yielded two driving trends: the change in the social fabric and the rate of change. The associated uncertainties were:

- Will the changes in "social fabric" be "turbulent" or "healthy"?

- Will "rate of change" be "slow/resistant" or "rapid/embracing"?

Plotting these as axes gives four distinctly different worlds, shown as quadrants in Figure I.1.1.

SCENARIOS FOR 2010

With these quadrants defining four distinct scenarios, the scenario team and Global Business Network (GBN) then put flesh on the bones by drafting four narratives, describing the public education system in Seattle as it would appear to a visitor in 2010.

Mosaic
Upper left quadrant: Fairly high rate of change in a turbulent social environment.

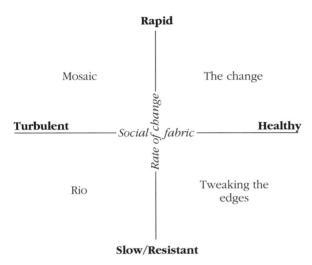

Figure I.1.1 Four scenarios for education in Seattle (reproduced by permission of Roger Erskine and Jay Ogilvy).

In this scenario, significant advances in technology and educational reform come to the few but not to the many. Riding a reasonably strong economy and continued interest in Seattle from other parts of the world, Seattle's citizens are too busy to worry about a comprehensive plan for education. Piecemeal reforms favour the best of schools while continued decay afflicts the worst.

Times were good in Seattle. The national economy was on a roll as well. By the late 1990s, the middle class was starting to gain real increases in disposable income for the first time since the early 1970s.

But Seattle's urban schools suffered a continuing slide into decrepitude. Old buildings, ageing teachers and dispirited students witnessed increasing violence in city schools. Behind the headlines about increasing numbers of crack babies, the remaining occupants of poor neighbourhoods saw the continuing flight of bright students and teachers toward the suburbs.

By the end of the scenario period, Seattle has become a city of enclaves and sanctuaries, some rich, some poor, but all in uneasy relations with one another. A sense of commonwealth has

13

somehow been lost. Real-estate values reflect sharp and abrupt differences among a mosaic of neighbourhoods whose diverse schools function as magnets for wealth or poverty.

The new mosaic of educational offerings has created a highly competitive, highly entrepreneurial atmosphere. Among the most innovative and widely watched experiments is the bold approach taken by the new principal at one school, a retired army colonel. The threat of violence among adolescent males was making teachers and other students wish for reinforcements; meanwhile, there were many adult males who were undereducated and under-employed. So the new principal decided to put the two groups together in mixed age, all-male classrooms. Blending experiences from Outward Bound and boot camps to apprenticeship pro-grammes and traditional classroom learning, he created a programme that allowed the older students to keep the kids in line, while the younger students gave their older classmates some experience in exercising responsible leadership.

Seattle has become a testing ground for educational experimenta-tion and, as such, the eyes of the nation are focused on its schools. Unfortunately, some experiments fail. And worse, those urban schools that remain untouched by the spirit of reform cannot claim the status of intentional "controls". They are sliding ever further down the slippery slope towards urban and educational decay.

Rio

Lower left quadrant: slow change, turbulent environment.

This scenario represents the worst case: Seattle's entire public school system slides into the morass that only a few schools entered at the end of the first scenario. Buffeted by bad times economically and unredeemed by energetic reforms, Seattle's public schools follow the pattern set by urban public schools in cities like Detroit, New York and Washington, DC.

First came the economic drought caused by America's mishandling of trade relations with the South-east Asian economies. Conflicts over trade with Japan were handled every bit as badly as conflicts over human rights with China. By pushing our own interests with each of the eastern powerhouses so strongly, we managed to push them together.

Second came the weakness of the local and domestic economies. Dragged down by Boeing's loss of sales to the other two Empires and weakened by the lacklustre performance of the American Empire, Seattle's local economy stuttered and stopped growing. Like Seattle's bridges, her schools as well went on a lean diet of maintenance while those in charge waited for tax revenues to return to normal. But they never did. The state stepped in to run the school system and parents redoubled their efforts. But, finding the state's bureaucrats even less responsive to influence than the former school board, many parents chose to remove their children from public schools.

For those left in the state-run public high schools, the curriculum looks like a cross between army boot camp, reform school and vocational training. Security is intense. Most schools have metal detectors and armed guards. Ethnic tensions are high.

This scenario concludes with a cadence of gunfire and the sound of breaking glass.

Tweaking the edges
Lower right quadrant: slow change, healthy environment.

*This is a scenario in which the economy creates jobs fast enough to keep the lid on any incipient social unrest. Never provoked to a boil, the discontent of the underprivileged simmers throughout the 1990s and no major reforms rock the school system. Driven by global economic forces and local demographic polarization, this scenario comes to a branch point: more of the same is insufficient. Depending on choices and conditions, this scenario leads either down towards **Rio** or up towards **The change**.*

The economic recovery that began in 1993 continued modestly throughout the decade. But, beneath the relatively calm surface, deeper forces in technology, demographics and the global economy were active. For example, as Saskia Sassen showed in

The Global City (Sassen, 1991), the influences of communications technology and globalization of the economy lead toward a two-tiered society. Growth of the financial and service sectors, in place of the globally dispersed manufacturing sector, creates high-paying jobs at the top of the economy and low-paying service jobs at the bottom of the economy, but few jobs for the middle class. As a global city, Seattle finds itself caught in the grip of an inexorable logic pulling her citizenry towards a two-tiered society.

A new body of theory, based on both domestic and international research, is beginning to show the costs of inequality, not just for the poor but for the rich as well. Studies of the Newly Industrialized Countries (NICs) of the Far East, as well as studies of income distribution in the USA, are converging on the insight that inequality hurts everyone.

So, for this scenario the question is one of whether inaction in the short term leads down towards *Rio*, or through some sort of crisis that inspires a transformation towards *The change*.

The change

Upper right quadrant: rapid change, benign environment.

This scenario represents the combination of rapid educational reform and technological innovation in the context of a benign economy and a healthy city; that is, it represents Seattle's best hope for a future in which urban education is saved from the course it has followed in so many of America's other cities. Can Seattle accomplish what no other city has managed? It depends on energizing forces from across the spectrum to form a critical mass.

Mayor Norm Rice's comprehensive plan, "Toward a Sustainable Seattle", didn't say all that much about education, so it came as something of a surprise when the city took over the school system.

City Hall was able to enlist strong support for educational reform among many segments of the Seattle community: parents, teachers, administrators and the business community. The Mayor appointed a blue ribbon commission including local and national authorities on education, psychology and new technologies.

Reading Seattle's newspapers, one couldn't help sensing an extraordinary turn towards the future, evident in the concern for the children, in the debate over the comprehensive plan and in a focus on information technology. More than most cities in the USA, Seattle seemed poised to lead the way into the information era. With the help of major grants and technology from Microsoft and US West, Seattle's schools were among the first to take full advantage of linking up to the information superhighway. Every classroom got telephone lines and modems to take advantage of the immense reservoir of educational resources becoming available over the Internet.

Information technology was not, as some had feared, an impersonal technology that would displace teachers and turn students into solitary nerds. Instead, the new hardware and software made learning easier, faster and much more fun than it had been for earlier generations of students.

The reforms were truly radical:

- Schools became community centers open all the year round, 14 hours a day. Health education, language labs and retraining for employment all took place in buildings that had formerly stood empty for months a year and many hours each day.

- Pre-school proved itself in research that showed the lasting advantages gained by children who learn how to learn very early. Seattle became a centre of research and development for education of children up to 5 years old.

- At the other end of the age spectrum, adult education thrived on the synergy between increased use of distance learning over the local area network, supplemented by face-to-face learning in all those classes that were now open at night.

- Funding followed students rather than going directly to schools, so different schools competed with one another for students and their funds.

17

- Now convinced of the importance of education for *all* citizens, rich and poor, urban and suburban, the electorate opened the way to greater funding for education.

- Business, too, took a more active role in public education, supplying teaching assistance from among its employees and jobs tailored to Seattle school graduates.

The citizens of Seattle seemed so adept at change by the turn of the century that other cities were sending delegations to learn the secret. How had Seattle changed everything at once with so little evidence of stress and strain? What those delegations found was an unusual willingness to take risks: a willingness to reward change without punishing the occasional failure; a capacity to learn from mistakes that were openly acknowledged; a mutual trust between unions and business; the successful use of conflict resolution tools that could be taught and learned. None of these innovations could account for *The change* by themselves, but all of them together, in systemic synergy, had transformed Seattle's education system from a creaky bureaucracy into a vibrant organism capable of growth and development, a system that truly served the needs of its students.

IMPLICATIONS AND CONSEQUENCES

Once exposed to a longer perspective, what implications can we draw from these scenarios and what were some of their consequences?

1. After the scenarios, Seattle passed two school bonds. Seattle got a terrific superintendent, John Stanford, who, precisely as it had been written in one of the scenarios, came out of the military. Enrolment has stabilized. Some schools have definitely turned round. There is a new can-do spirit, and the union is known nationwide as showing leadership on behalf of education reform.

2. We cannot expect every citizen to master the latest advances in

urban economics and telecommunications. But we can expect people to listen up to stories. Consequences of this set of scenarios were a deeper dialogue about education in Seattle and renewed interest on the part of the business community. People realized, "We have some choices".

3. While many of the forces operating on education in Seattle may have remote origins, Seattle's citizens *can* develop effective responses to national and global trends.

4. These scenarios suggest that Seattle's current system of educational governance is susceptible to administrative gridlock. Partly as a result of these scenarios, the union dropped its insistence on seniority as the main requirement for teacher placement. Schools in poorer neighbourhoods used to get the rookies while older, more experienced teachers went to the better schools. Now, there is a more even distribution of talent.

Rotterdam and Arnhem

These two case studies are based on conversations with Jaap Leemhuis of Global Business Network (GBN) Europe. They describe the use of scenarios to formulate options for citizens in order to understand their vision of a desirable future for their city and region.

ROTTERDAM

Rotterdam City Council wanted to mount a "50 year" celebration of rebuilding the city, and to hold the celebration in 1995. But, instead of looking back, they wanted to look forward. They decided to commission the design of a process that would engage the public in thinking about the future of Rotterdam in 50 years time. The city development department engaged with Arcadis's Jandirk Hoekstra who turned to GBN Europe for assistance.

The start was six evenings of "town meetings" held in the large church in the centre of the city, the Laurenskerk. Each was organized around a different dimension of the future (e.g. economic, social, public space, ecology, etc.) and was introduced by 30-minute contributions from experts, before opening the discussion to the floor. The meetings were videoed and taped, and used as the inputs to a Scenario Group of Professors. This group worked with GBN Europe to develop two scenarios.

One scenario was for Rotterdam to maintain its industrial quality and role as the largest port in the world and with all the impact that has on quality of life: the environment, traffic, etc.

The second scenario envisaged port activity moving "out to sea" with the city redeveloping its focus on services and amenities.

The scenarios were fleshed out by 30 senior civil servants during a workshop in the Hotel New York (previously the head office of the Holland America Line shipping company), and written up by professional writers and editors into a booklet that was widely distributed throughout Rotterdam. The scenario descriptions were then given to six architects who were asked to produce projects for city renewal that would be robust under both scenarios. The projects were discussed by the architects and the public at six open evenings at the Architectural Institute. They were also the basis of an exhibition that was open for three months, with visitors able to walk through the scenarios and projects.

ARNHEM

The Rotterdam example was in the mind of the city planners for Arnhem when they asked Hoekstra and GBN Europe to help their own planning process. Arnhem sits on the main route between the industrial Ruhr in Germany and Rotterdam. It is also a very beautiful part of the Netherlands, attracting many retirees. The question for Arnhem was: how to manage development?

Using a similar process to that for Rotterdam, the project kicked off with town meetings, held this time in the Musis Sacrum Concert Hall. One of the six evenings was devoted to the 'logistics hub' dimension of Arnhem's future since that is so dominant. The Scenario Group was made up of City administrators (including the Lord Mayor), and they developed four very different scenarios for Arnhem in 2015. The scenarios were presented in a booklet and each scenario description started with an introduction expressing the impressions of a visitor to the future. So, we view each scenario through the eyes of a young technician who visits the *Logistics Hub* world or a 75-year-old who evaluates the *Retirement Haven* future.

The City created a "Villa 2015", with each of four large rooms representing one of the scenarios. All Arnhem's inhabitants were sent a postcard picturing the four scenarios, inviting them to visit the Villa 2015. As they were leaving, visitors were asked to fill in a questionnaire on their preferences. The information gathered has since been used extensively by the city planners of Arnhem.

LESSONS LEARNED

The scenarios developed for Rotterdam and Arnhem both fulfilled their purpose: to provide a celebration in one case and to provide information to city planners in the other. In both cases, the scenarios provided:

- a crucial link in the process;

- a focus for engagement, enabling a public discourse;

- a way of dealing with complexity.

The scenarios were, as the examples made clear, a modest part of the whole project in terms of cost and effort. They were of use because the city leadership wanted to use them and did not have real or imagined constraints that precluded them taking account of possible futures. The Arnhem case provided a novel way of creating a process for citizens to input to the planning of their own town.

Mission and consequences in Bueren

Dr Alexander Fink of ScMI contributed this case study, which is reproduced by permission of Scenario Management International AG. It describes scenarios for the future of a region in Germany and the development of action plans based on them.

BACKGROUND

Towns and municipalities today need to operate in an environment that is undergoing lasting change:

- *Global competition* leads to municipalities facing a growing field of competitors. For many companies, the question about their location is no longer "Bavaria, Westphalia or Saxony?" but "Germany, Ireland, Czech Republic or Malaysia?"

- *Technological developments* – especially the "information technology revolution" – cause existing location advantages to lose significance while new factors like ICT infrastructure, an innovative climate or potential for cooperation with universities all gain significance.

- The *financial flexibility* of many municipalities decreases because increasing expenditure (e.g. for welfare aid) is out of balance with decreasing or stagnating revenues.

To face these challenges, municipalities and regions have to act strategically (i.e. they have to recognize opportunities and risks and react to them in time). Bueren Council called in representatives of the University of Paderborn and ScMI to advise and facilitate the nine-month process.

THE "LOCATION DEVELOPMENT PROJECT"

The city of Bueren has around 22,000 inhabitants and is located 25 km south of Paderborn in North Rhine–Westphalia, Germany. In the spring of 1997, the Council of Bueren decided to examine the future outlook of the city and its surrounding villages with the help of a development project for "location Bueren". The aim was to elaborate proposals for sustained prosperous development.

The project was managed through three organizations specially created for the purpose.

- *Location conference* in which, in addition to representatives from the Council and the administration, 30 inhabitants from different groups and associations participated. The location conference met as a whole three times to determine the fundamental milestones of the project.

- *Teams:* The members of the location conference were divided up into three teams "Economy and Work Places", "Living and Leisure Time" and "City Marketing and Town Planning". The main task for these teams was the important one of elaborating the details for analysis of the initial situation and the specification of action options.

- *Coordination committee:* A coordination committee consisting of four representatives of the individual teams, plus the Mayor and the City Manager, was given the task of bringing the results together. Additionally, the committee had a significant influence on the development of the future scenarios.

STEPS OF THE PROJECT

A strategy fit for the future must not just solve today's problems; it must also think about future development possibilities, to detect opportunities and risks and then derive concrete measures from them. This is why, as well as analysing the initial situation, ScMI proposed the use of scenarios using the methodology described by Fink (2000).

It was decided that location *and* external scenarios should be created: location scenarios would capture key factors specific to Bueren and external scenarios would paint pictures of the global environment.

The project was carried out in six steps that were mainly worked out by the coordination committee. The members of the location conference prepared specific parts:

1. *Analysis of the current situation.* The project started with a characterization of the current situation by the members of the location conference and interested citizens. This determined the importance of certain competition factors and the relative strengths or weaknesses of location Bueren in these. Both criteria were transferred to the competition-factor portfolio, which showed the critical success factors (high significance and weak position) and the strategic success factors (high significance and strong position).

2. *Determination of key factors.* For the creation of scenarios, it was important to take location factors (e.g. retail trade) as well as global factors (e.g. economic policy) into consideration. A total of 137 such *influence factors* were determined for Bueren. An influence analysis was used to examine how these factors were linked, resulting in 24 *key factors* (16 local and 8 global key factors) being identified. These key factors are influence factors of special significance for location Bueren.

3. *Projections of key factors.* Possible future developments of the individual key factors, so-called *future projections,* were determined in this step. The aim was to describe several alternative developments for each of the 24 key factors.

4. *Location scenarios.* Scenarios rely on combinations of the determined future projections that are consistent as possible. All

the projections of the 16 local key factors were examined for compatibility in a consistency analysis. A special scenario software program analysed possible combinations of projections and gave six consistent future images, each based on several similar combinations of projections. The projections dominating a scenario were used to describe the scenario in profile.

For location Bueren, six location scenarios resulted from this process plus discussions within the coordination committee and the location conference:

- *Scenario I: Bueren as a location with high quality of life.* Location Bueren develops into an attractive economic focus with high quality of life. The service sector, industry and information sectors, linked with it, become the driving force of Bueren's economy. Population grows and exceeds 25,000 inhabitants by 2010. Bueren's inner city centre develops into an area for quality shopping, which is highly regarded even beyond the city limits.

- *Scenario II: Bueren gets involved in global competition.* The global competition between municipalities forces the city of Bueren to effect an aggressive economic promotion that at-tracts and keeps new investors to the location through generous offers. The service sector, flanked by netbound in-formation services, becomes the driving force of Bueren's economy. The population increases to more than 25,000 in-habitants by 2010. Branches of major stores increasingly char-acterize the structure of Bueren's retail trade.

- *Scenario III: Wealth on the basis of retaining Bueren's trad-itional structures.* The growth of Bueren and its villages is based mostly on its traditional economic structure and the expansion of existing companies. The main emphasis of local economic promotion is warehousing. Bueren will have approximately 24,000 inhabitants by 2010. The inner city develops into a location for quality shopping, highly re-garded even beyond the city.

- *Scenario IV: Bueren as a "boom town" at the expense of its individual character.* Bueren develops into a boom town that will have approximately 27,000 inhabitants by 2010 because of new housing development and strong population influx. The service sector, flanked by netbound information services, becomes the driving force of this development during which Bueren loses its "traditional character". Local loyalties and public engagement decrease. Local public services are strongly limited. Traditional retailers have to close down and branches of chain stores increasingly dominate Bueren's retail trade.

- *Scenario V: Location dominated by stagnation and crisis.* The industrial economy in Bueren is stagnating. A lot of traditional companies are forced to leave or resettle in low-pay areas. Economic promotion is the responsibility of the highest representatives of the city. Stagnation leads to significant moves away from Bueren, especially among young people, and the number of inhabitants remains static at 22,000. Public engagement decreases, social conflicts arise and many people travel to larger cities and superstores to shop. This especially affects Bueren's city centre.

- *Scenario VI: Bueren as a location for information technologies.* Through regional economic associations and inter-municipal cooperation, Bueren succeeds in establishing itself as a favourite location for new information technology and services linked to it. The high quality of life leads to new housing development and strong population influx. This results in Bueren having about 27,000 inhabitants by 2010. Additionally, Bueren's city centre develops into a location for quality shopping, which is highly regarded even beyond the city limits.

5. *Combination of location and external scenarios.* The above scenarios are embedded in a global environment (politics, economy, society, etc.). *Four external scenarios* were created: (1) free markets, (2) sustainable development, (3) information

society and (4) crisis in a split society. These external scenarios were used by the coordination committee to analyse the strengths or weaknesses of the location scenarios. Typical questions that were put included: Is it possible that we can achieve a high standard of living (location scenario I) within free markets (external scenario I)? What location scenarios could appear if we have to face a split society (external scenario IV)?

6. *Development and implementation of the mission.* Analysis of the current situation (step 1) and the assessed location scenarios (steps 2–5) were seen as a basis for development of a mission statement and a location strategy.

Development of the mission
Analysis of current strengths and weaknesses, as well as interpretation of local and external scenarios, led to the decision to develop a mission statement on the basis of the scenarios I, III and VI. In addition to this, aspects of scenario II ("Bueren gets involved in global competition") were included because the occurrence of this scenario strongly depends on global developments and Bueren should be prepared for such an option.

> **MISSION STATEMENT: "BUEREN STANDS FOR A HIGH QUALITY OF LIFE"**
>
> *In 2010, Bueren and its villages are a location with a high quality of life that is characterized by strong public engagement, creative location planning and a prosperous economy. The citizens identify with their city and the local facilities. Honorary activities within a "new voluntariness" are an important part of location development.*
>
> ***Economy and jobs:*** *The Bueren area has a broad, healthy economic structure at its disposal. It is characterized by traditional growing companies and various striving start-ups, especially in the service sector and in the area of information*

technology. *An essential part of the prosperous development is performed by a strategically acting economy promotion that also plays an active role in inter-municipal co-operation. The unemployment rate is significantly lower than that of the state or country.*

City development and infrastructure: *Including the development of new living areas and further influx, Bueren has an increase in population that is higher than that of the state or country. In the year 2010, Bueren has more than 25,000 inhabitants. A main emphasis in city development is Bueren's city center. The social peace is secured because the present strengths of the local infrastructure – schools, health service, quality of the environment, sport facilities and clubs – can be kept up and adapted to the growth. Attractive cultural and leisure time facilities are at the disposal of groups of all ages. Foreigners and immigrants are integrated in daily life and cultivate their traditions with each other and in associations.*

City planning, retail trade and traffic: *The continuous co-operation of citizens, municipal politics and economy within the model "Private-Public-Partnership" turns Bueren into a shopping and service location that is highly regarded, even beyond the city limits. A good infrastructure is given in all means of transport (road, rail, air) – also in regional public transport. A good connection to the adjoining regions Paderborn, Hochsauerland and Soest/Lippstadt is provided. Innovative traffic concepts secure the necessary connection of towns to the center and the inner-city traffic.*

Bueren City Council is a service organization that is strong in performance and offers a spectrum of municipal services corresponding to the changing needs of its citizens. The citizens have a positive overall view of their city that they actively transmit to the outside. The exponents of administration, politics, economy and public life promote – supported by active city marketing – the positive image of the location and by this contribute to the identification of the city.

Implementing the mission

Implementation of the mission statement is being carried out by means of a set of consequences and measures. *Consequences* describe what should basically be done to achieve the target position pictured in the mission statement. The first consequences were strengthening civil involvement and increasing the quality of housing as integral parts of improving the quality of life and establishing the image of a dynamic and modern municipality.

These relatively general consequences led to 30 concrete *measures* that were proposed by the specific teams and put together by the coordination committee.

One named person from Bueren has each taken responsibility for one of these measures. An example of such a measure is the proposed "Foundation Bueren":

Many innovative projects for location development can be more easily effected outside the existing, often very formal structures. "We from Bueren for our city" should be the motto of a "Foundation Bueren" which has yet to be founded. The generic aim should be the support of the civil engagement. The various activities of "Community Foundations" in the USA, as well as similar approaches in Germany, are examples of this. As an independent organization set up for the benefit of the public, the task of "Foundation Bueren" should be to collect donations from a broad spectrum of supporters (donations, foundations, funds, gifts) and to distribute them so that Bueren's important needs can be satisfied. Here the chairperson of the city conference of Bueren is responsible.

The whole process was supported by the local newspapers, and all results are visible to the public. One main effect is that political rivalries are reduced by a common understanding of alternative possible futures for location Bueren, and the development of alternative strategic options by representatives from across the political spectrum.

Scottish Enterprise's use of scenarios

This account has been written by Jonathan Star of Scottish Enterprise, with inputs from Robert Whyte of Scottish Enterprise and Eamonn Kelly of GBN. It is reproduced by permission of Jonathan Star, and more information may be found on the website, www.scottish-enterprise.com. It describes the use of scenarios to develop regional competitiveness.

BACKGROUND

Scottish Enterprise (SE) is the main public sector economic development agency in Scotland. Throughout the 1990s, its stated goal was to help generate jobs and prosperity for the people of Scotland. It is the means by which much of the government's economic development policy has been developed and implemented.

But the model of an economic development agency, its activities and its relationship with government and customers has changed markedly over the past two decades. In the 1980s, economic development was largely about alleviating the worst effects of the structural changes in the Scottish economy. Policy was concentrated on inward investment and property development in declining areas of Scotland. The role of the economic development agency was to do this: visibly to help affected areas by attracting new companies and regenerating localities.

Over the last decade, attention has switched to other sources of regional competitiveness. SE is now much more focused on the needs of business, and puts greater emphasis on the development of human and intellectual capital within the region. This is a reflection of the structural changes at work in our economy: the well-documented advent of the "knowledge economy" emerging and co-existing with the well-established "industrial" economy.

More fundamentally, policy makers have realized that the problems and opportunities encountered in Scotland cannot be solved by either government or private sector organizations acting alone. Scottish Enterprise had to work in partnership with others to deliver its overall goals. It still delivers many projects itself, but it has moved towards becoming an organization that seeks to connect players together and to facilitate broad-ranging solutions to problems.

So, two related challenges presented themselves: *"How could SE communicate the changing nature of the technological, economic and societal challenges Scotland faced?"* and *"How could we get ourselves, our partners and customers to understand that we all had to adjust our behaviours as a result?"*

One answer was to invest time and effort in strategic thinking, and scenarios were a major part of this.

DEVELOPING SCENARIO THINKING WITHIN SE

The Strategic Futures Team
The real impetus to scenario thinking within SE was the creation of the Strategic Futures Team (SFT) in late 1996. Previously, most of the strategic planning had taken place within a larger Strategy Group, who also had responsibility for operational research and evaluation, business planning and communications. Breaking up the group and, in so doing, creating SFT meant that a small team had the space and resources to challenge SE into thinking about the longer term implications of change. The feeling at the time was one of excitement and exploration. We were in new territory – trying to apply the theory of strategic thinking to the future of economic development. It worked for many people, but not for others who felt that the creation of such a team led to an "ivory tower" approach and did nothing to embed futures thinking across the whole of SE.

SFT, led by Eamonn Kelly, set out by pulling together a

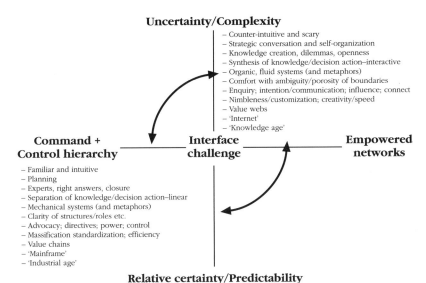

Uncertainty/Complexity

– Counter-intuitive and scary
– Strategic conversation and self-organization
– Knowledge creation, dilemmas, openness
– Synthesis of knowledge/decision action–interactive
– Organic, fluid systems (and metaphors)
– Comfort with ambiguity/porosity of boundaries
– Enquiry; intention/communication; influence; connect
– Nimbleness/customization; creativity/speed
– Value webs
– 'Internet'
– 'Knowledge age'

**Command +
Control hierarchy** — **Interface
challenge** — **Empowered
networks**

– Familiar and intuitive
– Planning
– Experts, right answers, closure
– Separation of knowledge/decision action–linear
– Mechanical systems (and metaphors)
– Clarity of structures/roles etc.
– Advocacy; directives; power; control
– Massification standardization; efficiency
– Value chains
– 'Mainframe'
– 'Industrial age'

Relative certainty/Predictability

Figure I.4.1 Using scenarios to understand organizational change (reproduced by permission of Jonathan Star).

presentation that challenged our colleagues to think differently about our changing world. We talked about the *knowledge economy* long before it became common currency in policy-making circles. That presentation, in various forms, was used over a hundred times. It became a very powerful means of telling and retelling a challenging story. And it has changed the language of Scottish Enterprise. For example, we contrasted the typical models and processes associated with the industrial economy with those emerging in the knowledge economy and mapped this on to a 2 × 2 matrix (see Figure I.4.1). Conventional, existing models became known as 'bottom-left' while emerging, more flexible models were 'top-right'. This terminology is still in use today, some five years after its introduction.

This example also indicates how scenario thinking was introduced to the organization. The bottom-left/top-right models were not presented as alternatives, but as equally likely possibilities that could coexist in the future. In this standard presentation, we advocated the use of more in-depth scenario-planning exercises

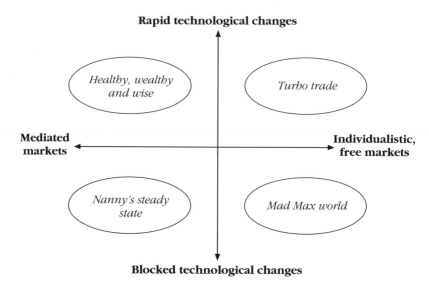

Rapid technological changes

Healthy, wealthy
and wise

Turbo trade

**Mediated
markets**

**Individualistic,
free markets**

Nanny's steady
state

Mad Max world

Blocked technological changes

Figure I.4.2 The brainspotting scenarios (reproduced by permission of
Jonathan Star).

as vital tools to help understand the nature of the changes we saw
around us.

At the same time, we invested heavily in training staff in the use
of scenario-planning techniques. These skills were then used to run
events with staff, customers and partners, to introduce them to the
ideas lying behind scenarios. Many of those trained have now
progressed to influential positions within SE, which suggests that
scenario thinking will play a valuable role in SE strategic processes
in the future.

As an example, one such event was with our major operational
teams within head office. In it, we created the *brainspotting*
scenarios (Figure I.4.2). With the help of colleagues from Global
Business Network (GBN), we created four scenarios that described
different ways in which the UK and world socio-economy could
develop. These were widely shared within SE, and we used some
novel ways of getting messages across – using theatre companies to
develop dramas based on the scenarios.

In August 1997, we used dramatized versions of the scenarios to
present to key companies in information industries (electronics,

software, optoelectronics, etc.) in Scotland. The idea was to engender a sense that companies, and industries, needed to take control of their own destiny in the future. SE's role was not to slow down change, but to equip Scottish companies with the information, techniques and mindsets to enable them to think strategically. By presenting to an industry group, it was hoped that the industry network would be engaged to take the thinking forward. And, in fact, the "cluster approach" developed within SE at this time used scenarios very heavily in trying to bring firms and individuals together. The Scottish food and drink industry has used a number of futures techniques (scenarios, visioning, learning journeys) to embed a sense of shared understanding and vision within the industry.

USING SCENARIOS WITH CUSTOMERS AND PARTNERS

The 'Scotland's Future' project
The ideas presented within SE were starting to reach a wider audience. People were becoming aware of models of visioning and scenario thinking that were happening around the world, such as the Mont Fleur Scenarios (Kahane, 1997). There were new, similar initiatives being set up within Scotland. But many were not coordinated. Scottish Enterprise imagined a situation where many of Scotland's key decision makers were engaged in a "civic dialogue", raising awareness of the opportunities and challenges raised by the emerging knowledge economy. As a result, in 1998 we pioneered the *Scotland's Future* (SF) process. Based on work done at a local level in Scotland and best practice from across the world, the SF process engaged around a thousand people across Scotland in discussions about the type of country they wanted to live in.

The process encompassed three themes: innovative organizations, sustainability, and creativity. Each theme was led by a high-profile member of a partner organization, with SE support. They were encouraged to use any of a variety of techniques, including scenario planning, to be visionary and innovative in their thinking about their area. In addition, the SF process encompassed a series of related events with world-renowned speakers; the Scenarios for Scotland process (see S4S below) and processes of community and on-line dialogue, including open-space events.

By early 1999, the momentum developed in the previous year had largely dissipated. The Scottish Council Foundation, commissioned to review the process, observed the following learning points:

- Many participants had been unsure of whether the dialogue processes were about the future of Scotland or of Scottish Enterprise. In their objectives for the process, SE clearly articulated that they saw the value coming from a greater strategic understanding between themselves and key economic development partners. However, the fact that SE was reviewing its own strategy at the same time, and did indeed look to the SF dialogue for wider perspectives, did lead to some confusion about objectives.

- Some participants had assumed that the process was one of dialogue with government, so their input became largely one of influence and lobbying.

- There was a widespread assumption that it was SE's responsibility, having convened the dialogue, to implement the ideas raised and find solutions. Although emphasis was put on the inclusive nature of the process, SE was still faced with questions like: "What are you going to do about it?"

- The convergence of the process into a large, set-piece conference gave the impression that the dialogue process was over and that action would begin. When this did not happen, many lost faith in "futures-thinking".

However, many positive aspects did come out of the process. It seems clear that joint strategy setting and action planning has become much more prevalent in Scotland over recent years. New forms of community involvement and strategic dialogue have emerged. Based on its previous experience, SE has encouraged and advised many of these initiatives.

SCENARIOS FOR SCOTLAND (S4S)

This project had its origins in discussions between St Andrews Management Institute and Scottish Enterprise in 1992. After many iterations, the project took shape in 1997, prompted by the announcement in June 1996 of a referendum on devolution. The focus was:

What sort of Scotland should the new devolved country be?

The project was sponsored by 10 organizations with interests in Scotland, including SE, and was managed by the Universities of St Andrews and Strathclyde. The 10 organizations had a variety of reasons for being involved. Some were organizations with headquarters in England wanting to build Scottish networks, others were organizations based in Scotland. All had some form of commercial or operational interest in understanding how Scotland might develop.

The project was very ambitious from a technical point of view. It used three methodologies to collect input and move to synthesis. They were:

- conventional interviews as in the Shell methodology;

- group interviews;

- use of the Decision Explorer groupware (see Part III.5).

The project was also very ambitious in scope. The sponsors plus two universities constituted a very large number of stakeholders to "keep happy" at all points in time. Given the subject area for discussion – the future of Scotland – the number of ideas produced (about 1,700) was too large for easy analysis. From the interviews, there appeared to be very clear views about existing problems in Scotland, but there were weak views about any alternative futures for Scotland.

However, the process did produce some valuable output. The sponsoring organizations felt that the first scenarios produced contained some flaws in logic and assumptions that were at least questionable. For example, one scenario assumed large increases in EU investment into Scotland; this was a highly unlikely situation, as resources are increasingly more focused on EU enlargement in Eastern Europe. Similarly, the question of "Scottish independence" was deemed to be both politically contentious and of second-order relevance. As a result of deliberations by the sponsoring organizations, the main differentiator between the high road and the low road became the *spirit of Scotland.*

The intellectual property of the scenarios was handed over to the University of St Andrews. The project concluded with a seminar at St Andrews on St Andrews Day 1999 describing two scenarios for 2015: *The Low Road* and *The High Road* (McKiernan et al., 2000, 2001a, b). The *Low Road* was a scenario in which inertia had triumphed, the new parliament had failed to provide leadership and the economy suffers against competition from the EU and elsewhere. The *High Road* is a normative or visionary scenario, in which Scotland develops, as Finland, Denmark and Ireland have done, by specializing in quality of life and a high-value economy.

However, more important are some of the outcomes since the scenarios were published. St Andrews University have been concerned with the follow-through, and Peter McKiernan reports:

> *One of the main outcomes was the incorporation of the language of the scenarios into policy and strategy decision making at many levels in the economy. For instance, in appraising policy options we frequently hear the expression "that's a low road strategy, what about the high road?" We know this to be the case within the government policy groups also. More so, we hear from companies and sector groups "come and help us, we are well onto the low road, show us how to get to the high road."*
>
> *The three-method approach has proved very robust on further scenario projects (e.g. the scenarios for Tees Valley, for Jersey, for the ICAEW). We have adapted the Decision Support method,*

replacing this with more traditional group interviews using Delphi techniques and workshops. Another tweak has been the development of our web-based scenario approach, used to good effect in Jersey and now in Grampian (Scotland) for scenarios for rural economies where folk are dispersed. Undergraduate and postgraduate students at St Andrews have been instrumental in the latter development.

So S4S has informed our continuous development of scenario methodology as well as stirring the strategy/policy option language in Scotland.

OTHER USES OF SCENARIOS IN SE

But as well as these larger exercises, SE has begun to use scenarios as a means of supporting its "mainstream" activities. It has promoted the use of scenario planning to get closer to its customers and partners, and, in so doing, it aims to develop the strategic capacity of these organizations to deal with future uncertainties.

The *Futures Programme* was specifically designed to use scenarios – as well as other techniques – as a means of strengthening the strategic thinking capacity of Small and Medium-sized Enterprises (SMEs). Following a positive evaluation, the pilot has now been extended and the Futures Programme (see Figure I.4.3) continues to develop and network smaller companies across Western Scotland.

The Futures Programme taught powerful lessons and generated practical learning for individual participants. It enabled some to "grasp the importance of moving the business on radically, rather than just getting better at the same approach." It brought benefits for organizations, as they explained that "everyone seemed to have shifted their view wider and the change appeared long term and durable." The Scottish Council Foundation report also stated that participants "... became aware that it is pointless for them to try and predict the future but that they have the ability to plan for future change, whenever it may occur". This programme is now in its fourth year within Scotland. We have also extended the

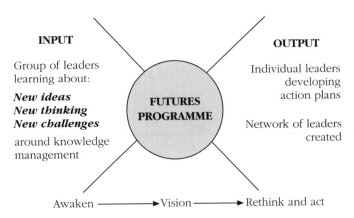

Figure I.4.3 The Futures Programme (reproduced by permission of Jonathan Star).

concept and applied it to working with some of our companies that have global aspirations.

Expertise in Scenario Planning has also become a vital route by which Scottish Enterprise develops relationships with partners. Because of the ability of our staff to conduct scenario exercises, we have reinforced a reputation of being "honest brokers" in bringing different groups together to discuss future-oriented issues. Over the last two years, we have played a major part in scenarios for the Scottish Tourist Board, Glasgow Housing Associations, the Scottish Consumer Council and the Scottish National Parks Authority. This final exercise was conducted with a group of people who had previously held very conventional views about the role of strategy and planning in decision making. Using scenario techniques allowed the group to develop a richer dialogue that discussed the future vision and role of the newly formed Loch Lomond and Trossachs National Park.

CONCLUSIONS

Scottish Enterprise has gained much from its investment in learning about scenario processes. Using scenarios has not been without its problems and frustrations, but it has helped SE develop an increased awareness of the wider forces affecting the economic future of Scotland. It has helped us to develop stronger relationships and networks within Scotland and overseas. It has provided direct benefit for many of our customers and partners. We will continue to use scenarios to help us in these aims. But more generally, in times of great change and uncertainty, we continue to see great promise in using scenarios to help develop Scotland's capacity for challenge, creativity and forward thinking.

Tackling big issues in 24 hours

This case study, taken from Ringland (1997), is included to show the value and design of 24-hour workshops in creating visions across cultures and providing a framework for action.

BACKGROUND

In the mid-1990s, the European Commission had a vision of Europe leading the world in adoption of information technology – in the "Information Society", and developed a number of programmes to pursue this vision.

However, there were considerable barriers. To explore how to overcome them, ICL hosted a scenario workshop at Hedsor, a country house, in July 1996 to address a number of issues:

- regulation in the light of new technological advances;

- the implementation of the Information Society in Europe such as public awareness/education, skills training;

- the most appropriate regulatory/institutional environment to encourage entrepreneurship and innovation.

Participants in the Hedsor seminar included Dr Martin Bangemann, then Commissioner for Industry in the European Commission, Keith Todd (then ICL's Chief Executive Officer), and 20 participants from the media and the Open University, public administration, telecoms and computing, and entrepreneurs. The workshop was facilitated by Peter Schwartz of GBN, and the participants represented 13 countries. The format of this event was very successful and has been used many times since.

SCENARIO THINKING TO HELP REDUCE FEAR, UNCERTAINTY AND DOUBT (FUD)

Table I.5.1 Agenda for a 24-hour workshop (Ringland, 1997; reproduced by permission of John Wiley & Sons, Ltd; source: ICL)	
Location:	Country House or other location removed from pressures
Players:	Owner: person who is hosting the event and is expecting recommendations from the Group Facilitator: in charge of process
Size of group:	Up to about 30 to have good group dynamics, more than 10 to get diversity of interests
Agenda:	Start late p.m. Introductions and agree aims Presentations – defining the terms Round table discussion after dinner Next morning, syndicate work (a maximum of four syndicates) on aspects of the question (e.g. for the Futurescope event [see below], the groups tackled work, education, leisure and the family) Create a picture of the desirable future Create a view of what happens if nothing changes (or, as in the Hedsor event, the undesirable future) Informal lunch or lunch with visiting speaker In plenary, syndicate groups report back using hand-written (or computer captured) summary points on foils Syndicate groups brainstorm actions and Recommendations In plenary, agree on actions, recommendations All participants take away hard copy of summary points and actions/recommendations.

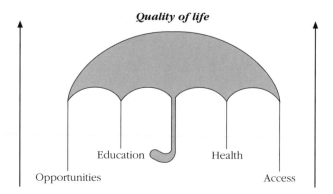

Figure I.5.1 Vision for Europe – a leading scenario (Ringland, 1997; reproduced by permission of John Wiley & Sons, Ltd; source: ICL).

LEADING AND TRAILING SCENARIOS

As part of the discussions, the group developed two visions for Europe: a leading and a trailing scenario (Figure I.5.1).

The leading scenario described a society with an improved quality of life. Contributing to that would be: opportunities for employment rather than jobs as such, opportunities for education, choices over lifestyle, health and medical care, and choice to use information technology or not – based on there being no barriers to access.

There are a number of things that have to happen for this scenario. The first is infrastructure: it is said that the cost of building the information highway in Europe could be €67 billion. The second is attitude of mind, which should be about using technology to solve problems, rather than installing technology for the sake of it. Another essential element of this scenario was the private sector, which should contribute to the bulk of the €67 billion of infrastructure plus help create all the ensuing services. This scenario is based on a model somewhere between the US approach driven by the stock market and a highly government-driven approach. It could be called a financial breakthrough, where the banks and the financial institutions are prepared to take incremental risks to invest in this scenario for the future.

One problem in Europe is that many countries are heading for a

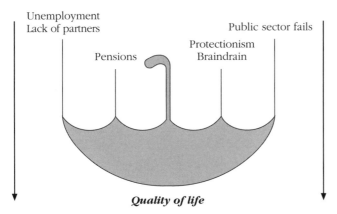

Unemployment
Lack of partners

Public sector fails

Pensions

Protectionism
Braindrain

Quality of life

Figure I.5.2 Vision for Europe – a trailing scenario (Ringland, 1997; reproduced by permission of John Wiley & Sons, Ltd; source: ICL).

huge pensions crisis. The only hope of solution rests with creating more employment to fund this yawning gap.

In the trailing scenario (Figure I.5.2), Europe fails to provide these additional jobs and opportunities, and there is a pensions crisis of astronomical proportions. Educational opportunities shrink, and hence potential new jobs do not emerge. Europe becomes the poor region of the world, with an exodus of talent, leading to fortress Europe mentality. The high standards of health and education that Europe now enjoys would shrink.

The group concluded that to achieve the leading scenario three elements had to be in place:

- The capacity of Europe to improve the relationship between entrepreneurship, education and the financial system.

- Education, helped by IT, needs to become a critical factor in growth in Europe, and Europe needs world-class companies such as a Microsoft of Europe. Overall, the whole attitude toward risk taking and management has to change.

- A new approach to regulation and deregulation in the light of technological developments. For example, while getting rid of monopolies is important, the completely deregulated model might not always be appropriate.

The group realized that formation of the Information Society represented as major a change and challenge as the formation of the industrial society, with the same or greater global implications, Europe could not isolate itself from the rest of the world. But there was still not enough awareness in Europe generally about the potential of the Information Society, although Europe's strength in education, literature, media and the arts means it could make an effective contribution. The entrepreneurial approach necessary to make European companies into global players was also missing.

The recommendations made by the meeting focused on areas for action which would use the infrastructure of communications, and which could be carried out over the next two years to take effect over the next decade. It was argued that attention should be shifted to spreading awareness of the impact of the Information Society from large organizations to individuals so they understand the potential to increase their skills, to SMEs that will play a critical role in advancing the Information Society by extending their global reach through technology, and to local governments as catalysts and providers of local networks with a bridge to global resources.

THE FUTURESCOPE GROUP

Following the Hedsor seminar, we were concerned that perhaps the Hedsor participants who were mostly in their 40s or 50s might have a systematically different view of life from the next generation, who would be living in the Information Society.

So, we invited a group of 17 young graduates from throughout ICL, from a wide range of backgrounds and nationalities, and with differing knowledge, skills, attitudes and experience, to attend a $1\frac{1}{2}$-day "Futurescope" workshop to consider Europe in 2006: What should we want and expect from the Information Society? After an initial brainstorming session to collect views about

Europe and the Information Society in 2006, three main themes were extracted for breakout groups to consider in more detail: work, education, leisure and the family.

It was concluded that there could be no single definitive picture of the Information Society in Europe in 2006 because too many uncertainties remain about what this society will look and feel like. The group decided that, although the uncertainty in itself does not necessarily have to be a bad thing – it can open up exciting opportunities – it would be useful to reduce some of the uncertainty and steer the Information Society in a certain direction. The discussion brought forth a number of predictable and uncertain factors to help in this "steering".

WHAT IS UNCERTAIN AND WHAT IS PREDICTABLE ABOUT THE FUTURE?

Leisure and the family
Uncertainties: Return to original values; fragmentation of social patterns, convergence of work and leisure; response to deterioration in the environment; the choice of home working; the re-emergence of the importance of religion and the censorship of information.

Predictable: Increased levels of travel for leisure purposes/activities; increased number of women in the workplace; social interaction with particular reference to the advent of technologies that reduce society's need to interact during certain activities (i.e. home shopping).

Education
Uncertainties: Society's attitude to education; the use of languages; cultural and social values; teaching skills; legislation; the role of parents and the funding of education.

Predictable: Integrity of information (information control); the advent of PCs and network computers; lifelong, self and distance learning; the Internet; understanding the capability of and exploiting IT; flexibility and the impact that commerce may have on education.

Work

Uncertainties: Style of leadership, ability of people to change, geographic boundaries and the effect of European politics on jobs; company loyalty vs. company change and commoditization vs. target markets (niche).

Predictable: Increased rate of change; new working roles and their complexity; change in the job mix and the increased importance of marketable multi-skilled employees; more women in the workplace; working smarter; increasing levels of competition; less interaction with colleagues; culture awareness and skills; the use of technology for communication and job insecurity.

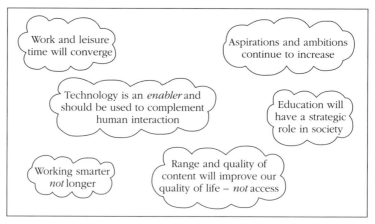

Figure I.5.3 Vision of the Futurescope Group (Ringland, 1997; reproduced by permission of John Wiley & Sons, Ltd; source: ICL).

The Group's vision of the Information Society differed from that of the Hedsor Group in one important particular. The emphases that they placed on leisure, on working smarter not longer, on education (see Figure I.5.3) were significantly higher.

At the end of the workshop, the Group made a number of recommendations.

● More information should be provided on EU discussions in all nations in a format that is easy to understand and read. This could be helped by a structured EU awareness/advertising campaign. Also, forums, particularly involving the younger generations who are growing up with the assumptions and aspirations of the Information Society, should meet to establish a vision of Europe.

- In schools and colleges, career advisors should actively promote the increasing need for a flexible workforce that is willing to and can accommodate change.

- In industry, companies should provide "management of change" training to prepare its workforce for the need for transferable skills and a flexible attitude. They should also make flexible working easier by offering the choice of working from home and providing the means (technology) to do so, and by measuring performance on realistic results, not hours worked.

- The younger generation should have a more valued role in the creation of the Information Society, in recognition of the fact that they foster different ambitions and approaches that are relevant to decision makers.

The output from the two workshops was:

- First, a short write-up of the event and its recommendations was posted on the Internet asking for comments and additional areas for action. The focus was on recommendations rather than the scenarios that had been used to develop the recommendations, though the leading scenario did start to create a vision of why and how we might enjoy an Information Society.

- Then a report, *The Hedsor Memorandum*, was written. It included comments from consultation on the Internet and recommendations from both groups; it was widely circulated to policy makers.

LESSONS LEARNED

- Cross-cultural groups of a similar age may share more attitudes than they do with a group of a different age but similar (Western) culture.

- A time frame of 24 hours can produce useful thinking but needs back-up work to tease out the nuggets from the discussion and manage the downstream implementation.

- Do not start a session when more than 10 people are present with any except the briefest of mutual introductions. Two minutes from each of 30 people is an hour, during which time people stay in their "day job" mode and delay innovative thinking.

Scenarios for sustainable development

This case study is based on the scenarios created by the World Business Council for Sustainable Development (WBCSD) in 1997. They encapsulate some of the choices facing a sustainable world, the effect that they have had not only on the 34 member companies but also in a wider context. The full scenarios are to be found on the Shell website (see Table III.1.1), and Ged Davis of Shell, the Project Leader, has provided an update on some of the uses of the scenarios since they were published.

BACKGROUND

WBCSD is a coalition of 150 international companies united by a shared commitment to sustainable development. The members are drawn from more than 30 countries and 20 major industrial sectors. The WBCSD also benefits from a global network of 30 national and regional business councils and partner organizations involving some 700 business leaders globally.

Their mission is to provide business leadership as a catalyst for change toward sustainable development, and to promote eco-efficiency, innovation and corporate social responsibility.

The project started with the Brundtland Commission's (United Nations, 1987) definition of sustainable development:

Humanity has the ability to make development sustainable – to ensure that it meets the needs of the present without compromising the ability of future generations to meet their own needs.

51

The project identified that three strands were important:

- economy and technology;

- governance and equity;

- ecology and demography.

And that they were embedded in values, myths and beliefs about society (see Figure I.6.1).
The key questions were summarized as:

- What are the critical thresholds in soil, air, climate, water and biodiversity, and how do we recognize these limits? How resilient is the global ecosystem?

- What human social systems can best respond to the challenge of sustainable development?

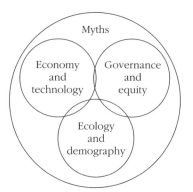

Figure I.6.1 Structure of sustainability (reproduced by permission of WBCSD, Geneva).

THE NEW, THE MANY, THE CONNECTED

The project identified driving forces that will persist and shape the business environment in any scenario. They were grouped under the headings of "The New", "The Many" and "The Connected".

The New relates not only to information and biotechnology, but also to new countries operating globally, new businesses and new organizations such as non-governmental organizations. *The Many* describes the continued growth in population, at least outside the developed world, and the increase in material consumption associated with increased wealth and aspiration. *The Connected* refers both to the speed and extent of our interconnection, and the problems that this raises for social and political systems designed for a slower world.

THREE SCENARIOS

These factors affect the answers to the key questions differently in each of the three scenarios. In the *FROG!* (First Raise Our Growth) scenario, based on current approaches to sustainability problems, the response is inadequate – human social systems are unable to meet the challenges and the ecosystem remains vulnerable. In the *GEOpolity* scenario, the response is to build an interlocking governance structure coordinated at the international level. In the *JAZZ* scenario, markets are harnessed for finding solutions to sustainable development.

By considering each scenario as a possible future world, challenges and lessons for business were drawn out.

The challenge to business of the *FROG!* scenario (Figure I.6.2) is

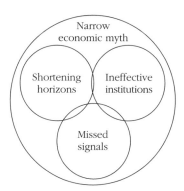

Figure I.6.2 FROG! scenario (reproduced by permission of WBCSD, Geneva).

"clean your spectacles", make sure signals get through, learn from other people, take "social" precautions. The lessons are:

• measurements for sustainability are needed, and need to be accepted globally;

• reading a broader set of signals is important (social and ecological, not just economic and financial);

• there is a lack of leadership and coordination between business and government;

• keep some institutions alive so that if you get a shock you can deal with it;

• in a low-trust environment, social costs could be shifted onto business;

• need to think "out of the box".

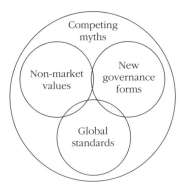

Figure 1.6.3 GEOpolity scenario (reproduced by permission of WBCSD, Geneva).

The challenge to business of the *GEOpolity* scenario (Figure I.6.3) is to contribute and where possible shape the emerging debate on new institutions and rules of conduct, and move business into a position of influence. The lessons are:

- address your social licence to operate;

- mark the importance of understanding government and new global institutions.

Figure I.6.4 JAZZ scenario (reproduced by permission of WBCSD, Geneva).

The challenge to business of the *JAZZ* scenario (Figure I.6.4) is to become involved early on in working with a wide range of stakeholders on environmental and social matters as competitive issues, in a more open and transparent world. The lessons are:

- you cannot operate against the public good for long;

- mark the importance of understanding the cross-fertilization of technology;

- the business of business is more than business.

SINCE THE SCENARIOS WERE PUBLISHED

- The scenarios have been used to provide a common language in which the member companies of the World Business Council for Sustainable Development can discuss the issues.

- They have also been used by the Council and some individual member companies for engaging with NGOs, the UN, The World Bank and governments.

- And, notably, the scenarios have been the basis of a major educational effort by WBCSD, their "Global Challenge" initiative.

- Overall, the scenarios have assisted organizations to take a more serious approach to sustainable development.

- They have also been the foundation for more focused scenarios (e.g. on biotechnology, energy and USA-specific policies).

VISIONS scenarios on the future of Europe

This paper was written by Jan Rotmans, Marjolein B. A. van Asselt and Philip W. F. van Notten of the International Centre for Integrative Studies (ICIS), Maastricht University. It describes the VISIONS project (1998–2001), financed by the European Commission (DGXII/Research), a ground-breaking endeavour in the development of scenarios and integrated visions for Europe. The project was a collaborative effort between nine research institutes from all over Europe, each contributing its own expertise. The VISIONS output is intended for decision makers, policy makers, socially responsible businesses, civic society entities and citizens who want to think about sustainable development and want to effect change.

PROJECT GOAL

VISIONS' overarching goal was to demonstrate the many links between socio-economic and environmental processes, and to improve assessment of the future through integrative evaluation of the consequences of these interactions for Europe and European regions. In so doing, VISIONS aimed to raise awareness of sustainable development by increasing the understanding of the many links between socio-economic and environmental processes and by assessing the consequences for Europe from an integrated viewpoint.

To achieve these ambitions, a variety of methods were used to develop challenging scenarios for Europe in an innovative and scientifically sound way. It was therefore decided to develop exploratory scenarios that investigate a broad range of possible long-term futures rather than to develop decision scenarios that primarily generate short-term strategic options. The scenarios would be highly divergent, descriptive (rather than normative) in nature, and integrate relevant social, economic, environmental and institutional dimensions. A unique feature of the endeavour was the use of multiple time and geographical scales. The final scenarios include staggered time intervals that reach 50 years into the future. Global developments provide the context for European scenarios and for three sets of scenarios for three representative European regions: the North-West UK (abbreviated to NW-UK), the Italian city of Venice and the Dutch Green Heart area. For such an exploratory exercise, the scenarios needed to be forecasting (rather than back-casting) in nature and describe the paths into the future, rather than simply the end state of a particular line of development. Emphasis would be placed on how the scenario stories unfold in order to explore the links between socio-economic, environmental and in-stitutional processes and their dynamic interactions over time.

An additional aim was to use the project as an experimental arena so that lessons learned from the process could help improve both scenario methodology and the policy-making process for sustainable development.

PROCESS DESIGN

The experimental objectives were:

- to test new and existing scientific tools and participatory methods for scenario building;

- the development of exploratory scenarios (rather than decision scenarios);

- to develop a framework for the integration of tools and methods;

- to evaluate consensus and conflict between the various perspectives incorporated in the scenarios.

Following on from these objectives a process was designed where formal techniques such as computer simulation models and sophisticated ICT techniques supported a participatory process in which intuition and "out-of-the-box" thinking were leading principles. Existing scenarios for Europe that address sustainability issues were compared to determine the added value of VISIONS. The comparison included breaking the collection of existing scenarios down into four clusters: economic growth scenarios, environmental protection scenarios, scenarios reasoning from limited policy action (business-as-usual scenarios) and pessimistic future outlooks (doom scenarios).

THE PARTICIPANTS

Much effort was needed to gather a group of participants sufficiently heterogeneous to achieve the desired richness as well as the desired variety of knowledge and perspectives for the scenario process. The participants ultimately involved in the European and regional scenario development included representatives from regional, national and international businesses, governmental institutions, NGOs and science as well as citizens and artists from a variety of EU member states. The participants' expertise ranged from transport, energy, telecommunication, environmental science and urban development to ICT, automotives, chemicals and water, for example. Similarly, the European scenario process was enriched by the participation of artists and the media. There was also a large range in the age groups of the participants. For example, in the case of the Venice scenarios, focus groups were organized with both young (schoolchildren) and older (60+) people in order to include radically different perspectives on the past and the future. In total, over 200 people excluding the project members participated in the scenario endeavour.

Regular switching between participatory and analytical tools ensured an adequate integration of expert and stakeholder knowledge. The regional and European scenarios were developed using different combinations of participatory and analytical processes. For Europe as a whole, a participatory process of mutual learning was used, based on the scenario approach developed by Royal Dutch/Shell. This so-called "storyline" approach combines knowledge provided by experts through lectures with "free-format" brainstorming by stakeholders. The ideas put forward by the experts and stakeholders were structured in a clustering and prioritizing process from which storylines were developed. Storylines are narratives that describe a sequence of events linked in a logical and consistent manner that provide unconventional paths to the future. These narratives diverge strongly from business-as-usual types of projection. The storylines produced by the stakeholders were aggregated to a limited set of common narratives. Then the storylines were fleshed out and enriched using two kinds of research material generated within VISIONS: a review study of existing European scenario studies and a trend study on global flows that might influence future developments in Europe.

GATHERING INPUT

In Venice, stakeholders were selected, with whom in-depth interviews and focus groups were conducted. In the interviews, stakeholders were presented with predefined draft scenarios based on specific metaphors of how a future Venice might look. The scenarios were adapted and further enriched using the interviewees' input. The analytical tools that were used included advanced information and communication tools for the graphical design and representation of the scenarios.

Relevant indicators were selected in a first stakeholder workshop in the Green Heart area, from which a spatially explicit simulation model for the Green Heart area was constructed, using a cellular automata model that enables dynamic spatial trends to be explored and visualized at the regional level. A second workshop, was devoted to the development of storylines. These were enriched in the weeks following the workshop where the spatial patterns associated with the storylines were explored with the model. The draft scenarios and simulation experiments with the model were later discussed with the stakeholders who participated in the project.

Thematic workshops and gaming exercises were used in the NW-UK scenario development process. Prefabricated scenarios were discussed with stakeholders. Furthermore, a prototype of a NW-

Table I.7.1 VISIONS scenarios

Europe	NW-UK	Venice	Green Heart
Big is beautiful?	Market rules	City Machine	Water guiding
Knowledge is king	Management takeover	Cyberia	Technology rules
Convulsive change	Risk society	Gotham city	Leading Europe
	Sustainable communities	Venice Inc.	

UK model was developed and used. The notion of sustainable development as a long-term target for NW-UK has been extensively discussed among a wide group of stakeholders in recent years. This same group of stakeholders participated in the VISIONS project.

All these processes ultimately resulted in a range of scenarios: four for the NW-UK and Venice, and three for the Green Heart area and Europe (see Table I.7.1). A concerted effort was made to ensure that events and processes in the scenarios did not appear or disappear out of the blue. This meant paying particular attention to tying up loose ends and filling gaps in the plot of the stories.

SCENARIO CONTENT

The variables included in the scenarios are diverse in nature and number 12 in total. Of these variables, the *factors* are: equity, employment, consumption and environmental degradation. The *sectors* are: water, energy, transport and infrastructure. The *actors* are: governmental bodies, NGOs, businesses and scientists.

Chain scenarios[1] describe paths to the different European and regional futures. The scenarios were developed from qualitative stakeholder input and then underpinned with quantitative

---

[1] Chain scenarios are like films. They describe paths of development to the future. Snapshot scenarios are like photos. They merely describe the end state of a path of development.

information where deemed appropriate. However, the marrying of qualitative and quantitative data proved difficult with at times unsatisfactory results. The difficulties confirmed the fact that integration of the two types of data remains a methodological challenge.

The scenario dynamics are divergent, thanks in part to the diversity of the stakeholder-based input and the extensive use of participatory techniques. The divergent nature can also be attributed to the inclusion of action–reaction mechanisms and structural breaks in paths of development. The action–reaction mechanisms counter the tendency of many scenarios to merely extrapolate from the past and present and exclude deviations from a particular line of development. The participatory and qualitative elements helped develop divergent scenarios through the incorporation of structural and often sudden breaks with particular paths of development. These structural breaks were referred to as bifurcations and examples in the European scenarios include extreme climatic change and the failure of European integration. Bifurcations are presented next to the scenarios and act as teasers to stimulate the imagination.

FROM SCENARIOS TO INTEGRATED VISIONS

The final innovative step in the process involved integration of the regional and European scenarios into *integrated visions*. These visions are narratives that describe the complex patterns that emerge from the dynamics caused by action–reaction patterns, and that are overlooked in any single-scale scenario study. Integrated visions help to assess complex dynamics and to identify conflict and consensus between different scales and perspectives.

The framework of an integration methodology was developed at the start of the project. The approach was further determined during the course of the development process as the scenarios took shape. Scenarios were compared in terms of tensions and similarities. This comparative analysis was used to filter out a sensible selection of 144 possible combinations. Interesting combinations of dynamics between Europe and the regions and interregional interactions that cannot be seen at a single level were explored further in a workshop with the VISIONS partners. Two *similarity quartets* and one *tension quartet* were selected following the filtering and exploration of the combinations. The respective quartets indicated harmony and conflict between regional and European interests.

It was decided to write the visions from a retrospective vantage point. This meant examination of 50 years of dynamics and, taking 2050 as the point of departure, allowed multi-causality and quasi-surprises to be described in an understandable manner. Furthermore, the concept of *complexity syndromes* was introduced to illustrate complex dynamics. Complexity syndromes are consistent and logical narratives that develop from an event or combination of events; they indicate the complex course of action–reaction patterns over time.

INSIGHTS

The challenge for European sustainable development is to understand the complexity of European futures so that we are prepared for the *unthinkable*. The VISIONS project contributed to this understanding by designing a process of envisioning and by describing and analysing the future by means of regional and European scenarios and integrated visions (Rotmans et al., 2000; Rotmans et al., 2001).

The insights address institutional arrangements and the need to challenge dominant paradigms:

- *The importance of a long-term view:* What seem to be promising or optimal choices in the short term might turn out to be suboptimal or even destructive in the long term. These problems occur because short-term actions can produce lock-ins that prevent or dismiss potential structural measures and investments.

- *The importance of institutions and governance:* Current institutional settings do not allow the management of complexity towards sustainability. New societal arrangements (institutional innovation) that operate on different geographical levels include multiple actors and the need to be flexible enough to adapt to new circumstances. Institutional change is a prerequisite for sustainable development.

- *The evolution of mental frames of reference:* The process vs. the product: the envisioning process is just as important as the visions themselves, but both are necessary to disseminate insights in a successful manner. Through the envisioning process and the ongoing dynamics in the real world, issues that were ignored or played down might surface as key issues. This, in turn, influences agenda setting and prioritizing, not only in the real world but also in the scenario endeavour.

There is a VISIONS website that contains a wealth of downloadable material: www.icis.unimaas.nl/visions. *An assessment of recent European and global scenario studies including VISIONS is the focus of The European Environment Agency and ICIS's Cloudy Crystal Balls:* http://reports.eea.eu.int/Environmental_issues_series_17. *Lastly, Van Notten and Rotmans' article "The future of scenarios" presents a typology for scenarios and uses it to compare VISIONS with a number of other recent scenario projects (Van Notten and Rotmans, 2001).*

Foresight Futures 2001

This case study is an extract of the Foresight Report written by Frans Berkhout and Julia Hertin (Berkhout and Hertin, 2001). It is Crown Copyright and published by permission of the UK Department of Trade and Industry. It describes the development and use within government of a set of fairly simple scenarios that provide a framework for thinking about the future. Extracts from this report are also found in Sections III.1. III.2 and III.6 on the methodological aspects of scenarios.

INTRODUCTION

Foresight is a way of thinking about the future, of identifying opportunities in technologies and markets that could arise over the next 20 years. It brings business, academia and government together to answer questions such as:

- Where will future market opportunities lie?

- What research and action needs to take place now to ensure that UK business is in a strong position to make the most of these future opportunities

- What are the social and quality of life implications of this?

Envisioning possible futures is therefore central to Foresight. These futures scenarios provide the context for thinking about how the future could look and are the stimulus for debate that leads companies and organizations to think about and develop better strategies for the future. Many aspects of organizations' futures are well defined and within their control. However, in an increasingly fast-moving and complex world, there are also significant uncertainties about the future shape of markets, governance and social values that will have an important impact on organizations. There is also the increased risk of sudden, unexpected events that have impacts across the board.

Scenario planning is a way of picturing and managing towards these uncertain aspects of the future.

This report sets out four futures scenarios developed to provide a broadly consistent framework for thinking about alternative trends in the UK economy and society. They aim to encourage a range of audiences – business, government and researchers – to use scenario techniques to improve decision making and strategy setting. Guidance on using the scenarios is described later.

The scenarios were developed, reviewed and revised over the last three years by a team of researchers at SPRU-Science and Technology Policy Research, University of Sussex, in consultation with stakeholders from business, government and academia. An earlier version of the scenarios was published as *Environmental Futures* (Office for Science and Technology, 1998).

The framework builds on an extensive review of national and global futures scenarios and draws on work of related scenarios exercises in Foresight and more broadly. The scenario storylines are informed by an analysis of current socio-economic trends, but they also introduce elements of novelty and change. The main criteria for the development of scenario storylines are consistency and plausibility. The full scenarios are on the Foresight website as referenced in Section III.1.

THE FUTURES SCENARIOS

Scenarios are not intended to predict the future. Rather, they are tools for thinking about the future based on four assumptions:

- the future may be unlike the past and is shaped by human choice and action;

- the future cannot be foreseen, but exploring the future can inform present decisions;

- there are many possible futures and scenarios map a "possibility space".

- scenario development involves rational analysis and subjective judgement.

The four futures scenarios set out in this report describe the UK between 2010 and 2030. The scenarios suggest *possible* futures, exploring alternative directions in which social, economic and technological changes may evolve over the coming decades. Scenario storylines are built from a simple and coherent set of assumptions about the main drivers of change in the future. While they focus on broad socio-economic trends at the UK national level, the scenario framework can be used to produce more tailored assessments of specific sectors and areas of policy.

The scenarios have been framed in the context of two underlying drivers of change: social values and systems of governance. These dimensions are taken as background conditions that define the specific features of each scenario (Figure I.8.1). The *social values* dimension takes account of social and political priorities, as well as patterns of economic activity resulting from them. At one end of the spectrum (*individual*), values are dominated by economic and political liberalism, the rights of the individual and the pursuit of personal freedom. At the other end (*community*), values are shaped by more communitarian ethics emphasizing social net-works and responsibilities, with a greater concern with common goods, social cohesion and sustainable development.

The *governance system* dimension represents the structure of political authority and decision making. At one end (*interdependence*), governance is increasingly distributed away from the national level; this is seen as occurring both upwards – to the supranational alliances such as the European Union and large

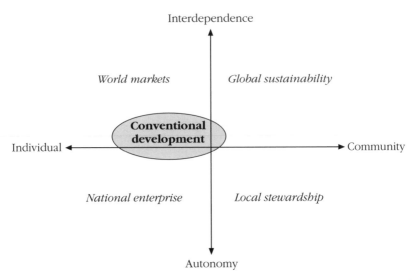

Figure I.8.1   Four UK futures scenarios (reproduced by permission of the dti; Crown Copyright).

international organizations – and downwards towards devolved and regional governments in the UK. At the other end of the spectrum (*autonomy*), decision-making power in public and private spheres is largely preserved (or strengthened) at national and regional levels, with political, economic and cultural boundaries enforced.

The scenarios are presented as storylines that set out some general trends and provide more detail in a limited number of domains: economic and sectoral trends; employment and social trends; regional development; health; welfare and education; and the environment. A synopsis of key drivers and underlying assumptions is given in Table I.8.1, Snapshot 2010. It provides key illustrative quantitative indicators for each of the scenarios. They were chosen to cover a wide range of economic, social and environmental issues and relate to commonly used statistics and indicator sets, such as the UK quality of life indicators (see Department of the Environment, 1999). All of the storylines and indicators presented here are illustrative. They are examples to get users on their way.

Table I.8.1   Scenario characteristics of Snapshot 2010 (reproduced by permission of the dti; Crown Copyright)

	World markets	National enterprise	Global responsibility	Local stewardship
DRIVERS				
Social values	Internationalist Libertarian	Nationalist Individualist	Internationalist Communitarian	Localist Cooperative
Governance structures	Weak Dispersed Consultative	Weak National Closed	Strong Coordinated Consultative	Strong Local Participative
Role of policy	Minimal enabling markets	State-centred market regulation to protect key sectors	Corporatist political, social and environmental goals	Interventionist social and environmental goals
ECONOMIC TRENDS				
Economic development	High growth High innovation Capital productivity	Medium–low growth Low innovation maintenance economy	Medium–high growth High innovation resource productivity	Low growth Low innovation modular and sustainable solutions
Structural change	Rapid towards services	More stable economic structure	Fast towards services	Moderate towards regional systems
Fast-growing sectors	Health and leisure, media and information, financial services, biotechnology, nanotechnology	Private health and education, domestic and personal services, tourism, retailing, defence	Education and training, large systems engineering, new and renewable energy, information services	Small-scale manufacturing, food and organic farming, local services
Declining sectors	Manufacturing agriculture	Public services, civil engineering	Fossil fuel energy, traditional manufacturing	Retailing, tourism, financial services
SOCIAL TRENDS				
Unemployment	Medium–low	Medium–high	Low	Medium–low (larger voluntary sector)
Income	High	Medium-low	Medium–high	Low
Equity	Strong decline	Decline	Improvement	Strong improvement
Areas of conflict	Social exclusion, immigration/ emigration, political accountability	Unemployment, poor public services, inequality	Structural change, change of skills, political accountability and institutional rigidity	Land-use conflicts, underinvestment environmental restrictions

FOUR SCENARIOS FOR UK FUTURES

World markets
People aspire to personal independence, material wealth and mobility to the exclusion of wider social goals. Integrated global markets are presumed to best deliver these goals. Internationally coordinated policy sets framework conditions for the efficient functioning of markets. The provision of goods and services is privatized wherever possible under the principle of "minimal government". Rights of individuals to personal freedoms are enshrined in law.

Global responsibility
People aspire to high levels of welfare within communities with shared values, more equally distributed opportunities and a sound environment. There is a belief that these objectives are best achieved through active public policy and international cooperation within the EU and at a global level. Social objectives are met through public provision, increasingly at an international level. Control of markets and people is achieved through a mixture of regulatory and norm-based mechanisms.

National enterprise
People aspire to personal independence and material wealth within a nationally rooted cultural identity. Liberalized markets, together with a commitment to build capabilities and resources to secure a high degree of national self-reliance and security, are believed to best deliver these goals. Political and cultural institutions are strengthened to buttress national autonomy in a more fragmented world.

Local stewardship
People aspire to sustainable levels of welfare in federal and networked communities. Markets are subject to social regulation to ensure more equally distributed opportunities and a high-quality local environment. Active public policy aims to promote economic activities that are small scale and regional in scope and acts to constrain large-scale markets and technologies. Local com-

munities are strengthened to ensure participative and transparent governance in a complex world.

WHY USE FUTURES SCENARIOS?

Society constantly faces change. Companies, policy-making institutions and civil society organizations can only work successfully and efficiently if they anticipate and take advantage of changing markets, technologies, public attitudes and so on. Organizations, as well as individuals, have a variety of ways of predicting and adapting to future trends. Why and when can scenario planning add value to strategy setting?

Although scenario exercises vary in their specific aims, they possess a number of common traits that distinguish them from more traditional forecasting approaches. Not only are they looking into the far future, usually one or more decades ahead, but they also assess developments across a broad domain. Confronted with large uncertainties about the future development of key driving forces, scenario exercises are based on the principles of *transparency* and *diversity*. Transparency refers to the process of making explicit assumptions about the relationships between drivers. Diversity implies that scenarios go beyond a single best estimate, or a "high" and "low" projection either side of this, and encourages us to explore a number of different, logically consistent pathways as a way of framing questions about the future.

The use of exploratory scenarios approaches should be considered when:

- discontinuous change is expected within normal planning horizons;

- the ability to adapt to future change is restrained, or if adjustments carry the risk of negative effects over the longer term (e.g. technological "lock-in");

- there are opportunities for positive gains from pursuing "robust strategies".

71

Broadly, the benefits of scenario planning are twofold:

- Scenario planning expands the range of future outcomes considered in strategic decision making. It promotes the development of strategies that are robust under a variety of circumstances, avoiding the risk of "putting all your eggs in one basket". It places the assumptions underlying strategic decisions under scrutiny; for example, about long-term growth prospects or consumer preferences.

- The process of engaging with scenario elaboration itself can be a valuable contribution to preparing the ground for change. If carried out in an inclusive and positive process, scenario planning can precipitate self-reflection within the organization, strengthen strategic thinking at all levels and help overcome organizational rigidities and routines.

HOW CAN THE FORESIGHT FUTURES 2001 SCENARIOS BE USED?

The Foresight Futures 2001 work can be used in a range of different ways depending on the needs of individuals or organizations and the resources available. Users are encouraged to develop their own conclusions about the futures, employing the scenarios as a starting point: elaborating and evaluating them in ways that are in tune with their needs. Over the past three years, a number of institutions have used the scenarios as a structured way of exploring the future. For example, a number of Foresight panels have attempted to identify future trends in economic sectors such as transport and energy; government departments have explored strategic policy issues and research; and research projects have used the scenarios to assess long-term socio-economic trends. Table I.8.2 gives a list of the Foresight Futures scenario exercises. Based on a review of these exercises and insights from the futures literature, this section provides guidance on the use of the Foresight Futures scenarios. It offers some ideas and recommendations, without attempting to be prescriptive.

Two fundamentally different approaches to the use of the scenarios can be distinguished. Most frequently, the Foresight Futures 2001 scenarios were used in small-scale scenario planning exercises, usually one-off events, that contributed to medium- and long-term business and policy planning. These processes are usually:

● qualitative exploration of trends;

● participative;

● based on the experience of practitioners;

● scenarios used as a communication tool.

Frequently, their use depends on a "champion" of scenario planning at a senior level of management. Their function is to attract interest and to stimulate creative thinking. These processes tend to engage participants who are unfamiliar with the scenario approaches and often unfamiliar with academic language and thinking:

> *An exercise carried out by the Foresight Crime Prevention Panel provides an example of a typical one-off scenario-planning event. The aim of the Panel is to explore the crime potentials of new technologies and to ensure that these potentials are minimized through preventive action. The Foresight Futures scenarios were used in a one-day workshop to structure thinking about the future of crime. Breakout groups organized around each of the four scenarios developed sectoral scenarios for the crime of the future. They identified new technologies that are likely to be used by criminals, potential prevention strategies and necessary responses. Results of the workshop were fed into the Panel's consultation paper and report (see http:www.foresight. gov.uk).*

The scenarios can also be used in the context of research-based studies carried out over longer periods. In these assessments, the main function of scenarios is to provide a heuristic framework that allows construction of a wider but still coherent set of assumptions. The method is used in very uncertain areas of research (e.g. climate change impact assessment). These uses are characterized through:

- qualitative and quantitative assessment of potential outcomes;

- scientific methods combined with consultation;

- data and expert knowledge;

- scenarios used to assess outcomes.

The main challenge for this approach is to combine the "soft" scenario tool with "hard", quantitative scientific methods. The report (Berkhout and Hertin, 2001) offers a number of indicators as an illustration of trends, but again these should only be seen as a starting point. If it seems appropriate, they can be revised, specified or complemented by other indicators. Simple modelling and cross-impact analysis can be employed to ensure consistency and analytical depth:

For example, the REGIS study on climate change made use of the Foresight Futures scenarios within the framework of an integrated assessment of potential climate change impacts. This study developed key socio-economic parameters for a number of sectors relevant for climate change impact assessment. The parameters were derived using the Environmental Futures scenarios as well as quantitative sectoral scenarios and forecasts available in the academic and policy literature. They provided the basis for running models of impacts in a number of sectors (e.g. water resources) as a means of assessing potential climate change impacts under different sets of socio-economic conditions.

Table I.8.2 identifies some of the uses of the environmental futures scenarios.

Table I.8.2 Overview of uses of the Environmental Futures scenarios (reproduced by permission of the dti; Crown Copyright)

Organization/ User	Sector	Aim	Type	Process
ACACIA research project	Climate change	Assess climate change impacts in the EU in 2050	Detailed, qualitative and quantitative	Based on data and expert knowledge, small team report/ EU policy
Regis research project	Climate change	Assess climate change impacts in NW England and East Anglia in 2020 and 2050	Detailed, qualitative and quantitative	Based on data and expert knowledge, small team report/ UK policy
Climate Change and the Demand for Water research project	Climate change and water demand	Assess impacts of climate change on water demand	Detailed, qualitative and quantitative	Based on data and expert knowledge, small team underway/UK policy
CSERGE, University of East Anglia	Climate change	Explore climate change impacts in East Anglia in 2002	Detailed, mainly qualitative	Structured stakeholder interviews report/regional stakeholders
Environment Agency, National Water Demand Management Centre (NWDMC)	Water demand	Assess levels and structure of water demand in 2025	Detailed, mainly quantitative	Based on data and expert knowledge, small team and consultation underway/UK policy and business
Digital Futures research project	ICTs and e-commerce	Explore the digital economy in 2010 and 2020	Detailed, qualitative and quantitative	Based on data and expert knowledge, small team and consultation report/ UK policy and business
Foresight – Crime Prevention panel	Crime	Explore issues of crime and crime prevention in 2020	Sketchy, qualitative	Participative workshop consultation document/UK policy and business
Foresight – integrated Transport Chain Task Force	Transport	Assess priorities for sustainable transport strategy	Detailed, quantitative and qualitative	Workshop, detailed elaboration by project manager report/UK Government

(*continued*)

Table I.8.2 (continued)

Organization/ User	Sector	Aim	Type	Process
Foresight – Energy Futures Task Force	Energy	Assess sustainable energy technologies	Sketchy, qualitative	Based on data and expert knowledge report/UK Government
Foresight – Minerals Panel	Minerals	Assess sustainability of minerals extraction and use	Detailed, qualitative and quantitative	Workshop report/ UK Government
Natural Environment Research council	Environment	Identify environmental research priorities	Sketchy, qualitative	Participative workshop report/ ENE Panel, NERC science policy
Cabinet Office Performance and Innovation Unit	Trade	Assess social and ethical issues in international trade	Detailed, qualitative	Workshop report/ UK policy
ESRC Financial Services Environmental Network	Financial services	Explore ethical and environmental impacts on financial products	Sketchy, qualitative	Workshop report/ financial services industry
Housing/Future skills	Built environment	Offered as strategic planning tool	NA	NA
Environment Agency	Environmental protection "visions" exercise	Element of corporate developed for nine environmental themes	Illustrative scenarios	Workshop input to early framing of Visions report

NA = Not applicable.

Lessons learned

The case studies in Part I have described the use of scenarios to develop public policy for regions or cities, countries, the environment. The lessons learned, as a result of the projects described in the case studies, include a number on governance and other wider issues than the use of scenarios. This list focuses on the use of scenarios while emphasizing the importance in any project of understanding the context and limitations of the scenario process.

CONTEXT FOR SCENARIOS

- The scenarios are often a modest part of the whole project, in terms of cost and effort. They are of use because managers do not have real or imagined constraints that preclude them taking account of possible futures (Rotterdam).

- Scenarios provide a crucial link in the process, a focus for engagement, enabling public discourse (Rotterdam).

- Scenarios provide a way of dealing with complexity (Arnhem, Foresight).

CREATING SCENARIOS

- The importance of a long-term view: what seem to be promising or optimal choices in the short term might turn out to be suboptimal or even destructive in the long term (VISIONS).

- The evolution of mental frames of reference: the envisioning process is just as important as the visions themselves but both are necessary to disseminate insights in a successful manner (VISIONS).

- Reading a broader set of signals is important (social and ecological, not just economic and financial) (Scenarios for sustainable development).

- There is a need to think "out of the box" in spite of the pressures for business as usual (Scenarios for sustainable development).

- Mark the importance of understanding the cross-fertilisation of technology. (Scenarios For Sustainable Development).

- Cross-cultural groups of a similar age may share more attitudes than they do with a group of a different age but similar national culture (Tackling big issues).

THE WORKSHOP PROCESS

- A time frame of 24 hours can produce useful thinking but needs back-up work to tease out the nuggets from the discussion and manage downstream implementation. (Tackling big issues)

- Do not start a session when more than 10 people are present with any except the briefest of mutual introductions. Otherwise, people will stay in their "day job" mode longer and delay innovative thinking. (Tackling big issues)

USING EXISTING SCENARIOS (FORESIGHT FUTURES 2001)

- Foresight Futures 2001 have been used in small-scale scenario planning exercises, usually one-off events, that contribute to medium and long-term business and policy planning. These are usually:

○ qualitative exploration of trends;

○ a participative process, often engaging participants who are unfamiliar with scenario thinking;

○ based on the experience of practitioners;

○ scenarios used as a communication tool to attract interest and to stimulate creative thinking.

- Foresight Futures 2001 has also been used in the context of research-based studies carried out over longer periods, to provide a heuristic framework that allows construction of a wider but still coherent set of assumptions. It is used in very uncertain areas of research (e.g. climate change impact assessment). These uses are characterized by:

○ qualitative and quantitative assessment of potential outcomes in which simple modelling and cross-impact analysis can be employed to ensure consistency and analytical depth;

○ scientific methods combined with consultation (i.e. "soft" scenario tools with "hard", quantitative scientific methods);

○ based on data and expert knowledge and, if appropriate, revised, specified or complemented by other indicators.

CLARITY OF RESPONSIBILITY

- In the Scottish Enterprise example, many participants had been unsure of whether the dialogue processes were about the future of Scotland, or of Scottish Enterprise itself.

- There was a widespread assumption that it was SE's responsibility, having initiated the dialogue, to implement the ideas raised and find solutions. Although emphasis was put on the inclusive nature of the process, SE was still faced with questions like: "What are you going to do about it?"

- The convergence of the process into a large, set-piece conference gave the impression that the dialogue process was over and that action would begin. When this did not happen, many lost faith in "futures-thinking" (Scottish Enterprise).

OUTCOMES

- People will listen to stories, and stories can promote a deeper dialogue and interest in civic affairs among citizens and the business community (Seattle, Rotterdam, Bueren).

- While many of the forces operating (on education in Seattle) may have remote origins, (Seattle's) citizens *can* develop effective responses to national and global trends.

- Scenarios can change organizational behaviour (Seattle, Bueren).

COMMUNICATION OF SCENARIOS

- Brochures and buildings in Arnhem and Rotterdam.

- Brochures and videos in Scotland.

- Email and website in "Tackling big issues".

- Brochures and websites (Scenarios for sustainable development, VISIONS, Foresight).

- Local newspapers (Bueren).

PART II

SCENARIOS IN THE PUBLIC SECTOR

SUMMARY

Many public and voluntary-sector organizations, like businesses, need to evaluate their strategic options as the environment changes. The case studies in this part describe scenario work primarily intended to develop strategy for organizations, wrestling with change, that happen to be in the public or voluntary sector. There are, however, differences between these approaches and those typically found in the private sector; they are highlighted and discussed later in Part IV.

The US GSA (General Services Agency) case study in Section II.1 describes how this organization, which supplies federal civil departments, used scenarios to rethink its vision in the world of e-commerce.

Section II.2 describes how Consignia, which runs the Royal Mail, has developed character-based scenarios for planning for new services.

Section II.3 discusses how, at the DTI (UK Department of Trade and Industry), imaginative use of visualization has been used to create an environment for discussing the future of government.

The problems of a voluntary-sector organization – the worldwide religious and teaching order, the Christian Brothers – provoked the use of scenarios to help think about a future in which the traditional members were no longer prepared to volunteer for the priesthood and the average age was increasing inexorably (Section II.4).

In Section II.6, the role of future studies and scenarios in public policy is considered, based on the author's experience in the Health Service and elsewhere.

Section II.7 brings together the lessons learned from the case studies; for instance, the need to engage with staff, the use of tools to create images and spaces for creating understanding, and the wider consultation and longer timescale of change in the public sector compared with the private sector.

US General Services Agency – scenarios for the Federal workplace

In January 2000, the General Services Administration (GSA) Marketing and Strategic Planning Division partnered with the Institute for Alternative Futures (IAF) to develop an in-house futures network, scenarios and "audacious" goals. The dramatic changes at GSA during the previous decade compelled the career leadership to recognize and plan for a future that was "different" from the institutional conventional wisdom. Thomas A. Skirbunt, PhD, Marketing and Strategic Planning, Office of Communications, GSA worked with Clement Bezold, PhD. and Jennifer Jang of IAF for a year, with remarkable results. While formal acceptance of particular scenarios remains elusive, GSA was able to produce draft scenarios and strategic goals that have helped revitalize the agency. This paper is in the public domain.

BACKGROUND

The US General Services Administration was created in 1949 as a centralized Federal procurement and property management agency. The primary objective then was to keep the overhead costs of the government as low as possible. It has since evolved from a mandatory supplier of space and supplies to Federal civilian agencies to a non-mandatory provider of all workplace-related systems and services to civilian and defence agencies. GSA's direct "customers" are other federal agencies and the private sector vendors with whom GSA contracts for goods and services. GSA headquarters are in Washington, DC but the vast bulk of its activity takes place in its 11 regional offices located in major cities around the country. GSA provides its customers with products and services through three traditional "stovepipe" organizations: The Federal Supply Service, The Federal Technology Service and the Public Buildings Service.

The 1990s was a difficult and challenging decade of change for GSA. The agency was significantly reorganized twice, and its staff reduced from 30,000 to 14,000. A number of significant procurements were criticized and its major court construction programme was denigrated as a pork barrel. As a part of the reorganization, all policy-making functions of the agency were consolidated into one new "Office of Government-wide Policy". For many in the agency, the future appeared to be a black hole.

In 1999, GSA celebrated the 50th anniversary of its creation in 1949. At the same time, GSA was largely responsible for the Federal effort to prevent a Y2K crisis as the new millennium dawned. This confluence of events generated an appreciation for the evolutionary change that was an integral part of GSA's history, and the craving grew for direction into the future. Simultaneously, for the first time, the agency's new strategic goals included the following:

> *GSA will anticipate future workplace needs. GSA will design, develop and model future Federal work environments with state-of-the art technology, innovation and best practices in use of space, furniture, equipment, telecommunications, contracts and other tools.*

The Marketing and Strategic Planning staff of the Office of Communication recognized that, in order to pursue this goal, a far greater understanding was needed of the economic, social, technological, etc. forces affecting the workplace than was available in 1999. The Strategic Marketing plan recognized the need for GSA to have an effective capacity for forecasting potential changes in the nature of work and workplaces and the resultant impact on the Federal workforce. GSA determined that it would develop forecasts and scenarios as part of this capacity building.

DEVELOPING THE SCENARIOS

Scenario development began with the identification of those workplace trends that were most critical for, or of greatest importance to, the Federal workforce. GSA and IAF staff conducted focused research of GSA documents, IAF forecasts and Internet-related material as part of this trend assessment. In addition, IAF staff conducted representative, but not random, interviews of GSA career executives for their "take" on these trends.

Four trends were found to have the greatest potential to affect GSA's mission:

1. e-commerce;

2. virtuality and expert systems;

3. telework;

4. privatization.

Indeed, there was a clear sense among GSA's top career executives that these four trends were very important to GSA's future. There was agreement that e-commerce would enhance the capacity of Federal agencies to buy and sell for themselves and expand GSA's capacity to do the same. The vision was expressed that GSA might need to be the first civilian agency to go 24×7 (i.e. non-stop operation all day and every day). But there was no agreement on where or how to assess this trend.

The same was true for all the trends: general agreement on the forces at work, but a lack of consensus on where to turn for authoritative forecasts of these trends, or for assessments of their impact on the Federal workplace. Telework was seen as a growing trend in the national workplace with the potential to reduce significantly the need for federal office space. But there was no evident place to turn to for information on how fast telework would develop, or on the variable impact this trend might have on different Federal missions.

Another force that GSA agreed was at work, not just in the US but also in other countries ranging from Australia to Holland, was competition from the private sector through the privatization of provider/procurement activities. However, there was no consensus on which activities were most likely candidates for such privatization. The same was true for the impact of virtual systems: virtual systems would undoubtedly replace many existing acquisition and procurement processes, but questions loomed large on which systems and processes would be affected, when and to what extent.

In short, GSA was aware of the forces at work for change in their environment, but lacked a framework by which to evaluate these trends. In order to provide this framework, GSA Communications and IAF staff spent three months doing preliminary work on scenarios for GSA's future and two additional months of research on workplace trends leading up to the Visionary Directions/ Audacious Goals Conference in June 2000.

THE SCENARIOS

Four scenarios for GSA's future were presented to the career leadership in June 2000: the Linked Stovepipe Model, the Enterprise Model; the Higher Value Enterprise Model; and the Horizontal Government Model. They were developed using IAF's archetypal and aspirational approach to scenario development. Table II.1.1 briefly outlines the characteristics associated with each of these four scenarios for GSA.

As part of the scenario development process, a training exercise on futures research was held with mid-level career employees from all of GSA's service organizations. More than four scenarios evolved from this exercise, but these four represented an effective set from among the spectrum of possibilities:

- the Linked Stovepipe Model is the implicit "official future" that extrapolates the present into the future;

- the Enterprise Model contemplates a transformation of GSA away from stovepipe organizations, organized around specific

Table II.1.1   GSA scenarios for 2010

Model 1: Linked Stovepipe Model

- Decline in GSA Federal customers.

- Changes allow GSA to provide services to state and local government.

- Partnership within GSA occurs on an as-needed, as-desired basis, either for specific customers or specific projects.

- No new missions, roles or responsibilities.

- Intense competition for our customers from the private sector.

- E-commerce as a means to promote the sale of products.

Model 2: Enterprise Model

- Breakthrough/opportunities for integration of product/service delivery.

- Customer is the focus around which GSA is organized and operates.

- Minimal change to organization structure.

- E-commerce used to create and support vertical B2B environment with federal agency partners.

- Unprofitable product lines and functions cease to be performed.

Model 3: Higher Value Enterprise Model

- GSA as workplace environment expert. GSA leverages for best design and best prices around space, technology and supply.

- All supply-chain functions are dropped as the cost of such transactions for anyone approaches zero.

- Primary mission is as preservationist, asset manager, green workplace advocate, equal-opportunity champion, etc.

- E-marketplaces with and between Federal agencies are managed by GSA.

(*continued*)

Table II.1.1   (continued)

Model 4: Horizontal Government Model

- The integrated approach to solving problems generates a federal establishment much different in organizational look and feel.

- Lines between what are currently labelled civil and military functions become blurred.

- Focus of government is on the integrated team approach to solving the specific problems and concerns of individual citizens.

- Government personnel is 50 per cent of current levels and distributed evenly around the country.

- Government agency websites, dot.govs, are interwoven with each other and managed by GSA to provide real-time data on all business transactions of the Federal establishment.

---

products and services, to form an integrated agency organized around customers and service delivery;

- in the Higher Value Enterprise Model, GSA evolves into an organization that manages systems and knowledge rather than products and services;

- in the Horizontal Government Model, the face and role of the federal government is quite different from the present, and, in this integrated government, GSA is the manager of all knowledge transactions.

USE OF THE SCENARIOS

The scenarios were used as major input for a day-long conference exploring visionary directions, at which approximately 30 of the most senior career agency staff from GSA central office and its regions were present. Facilitated by Dr Bezold of IAF, the conference used the scenarios to explore the future environment for GSA and to prepare the group to consider visionary directions and audacious goals for GSA.

Participants considered specific topics and forecasts in relation to the scenarios. Forecasts of the growth in e-commerce were viewed as portents of the Enterprise and Higher Value Enterprise Model scenarios. In fact, in the previous two years, GSA had aggressively moved to offer its products and services on the Internet, conducted auctions for surplus property online and developed a system where its customer agencies can review their space rental charges. The future could soon see a shift of additional transactions to e-commerce, as serious consideration is being given to how best to communicate real-estate information online. And at least one GSA leader noted that e-commerce might precipitate changes in the geographic organizational structure of the agency.

Forecasts of the changing workplace are symptomatic of the Higher Value Enterprise and Horizontal Government scenarios. The size of the ageing Federal workforce is expected to continue to decline. Coupled with the need for ever "smarter" space and an ageing inventory of historic Federal buildings under its stewardship, GSA will be challenged to provide adaptable workspace. Working with Carnegie-Mellon, GSA has established an adaptable workplace lab at its Washington headquarters to experiment with workplace architecture.

The most significant conclusion reached at the conference was that the existing Linked Stovepipe Model of GSA – the "official" present extrapolated into the future – could not and would not survive to the year 2010. This led to an extremely productive consensus on GSA visionary directions and audacious goals.

The shared group visionary direction of GSA was that GSA:

- transforms government by creating and facilitating excellence in government;

- becomes the best place to work;

- promotes outreach to its customers, the public and stakeholders through the establishment of a unified government Internet portal;

- is a trusted partner and provider of innovative tools;

- lives by the statement "Excellence through services, progress through people."

This process in turn led to a lengthy and provocative discussion on audacious goals for the agency. As the long list (Table II.1.2) shows, the leadership was not content with audacious 10-year goals. Many of the suggested initiatives were given 5-year horizons or less, suggesting that the group perceived the urgency of both the opportunity and the need for movement away from a status quo future.

Through consensus-building dialogue, the group consolidated around the following six audacious goals, as those most favourable for further review and development:

- by 2003,

   o 50 per cent of Federal agencies are developing their 5-year strategic plans with GSA;

   o all government employees have PCs/Internet access at home;

   o GSA is ranked as one of the top 25 places to work in the USA.

- By 2005,

   o GSA is the primary applications service provider for enterprise resource planning services to all government agencies;

   o GSA enables any federal employee to work anywhere, anytime with maximum capability.

- By 2010, all Federal agencies look to GSA as the provider of choice for all administrative services.

The leadership group then resolved to develop each of these audacious goals for presentation to the new administration that would be assuming leadership of the agency the following January.

Table II.1.2   Potential audacious goals for GSA

- GSA is the provider of choice for all civilian agencies by 2010.

- By 2002, GSA has established extranets with all its top 10 customers.

- By 2003,

   - all government employees have PC/Internet access at home;

   - GSA is ranked as one of the top 25 places to work in the USA;

   - all government subjects, information and services are available to the public through a single web portal managed by GSA;

   - 50 per cent of Federal agencies are partnering with GSA to develop their strategic management plans.

- By 2005,

   - 25 per cent of capital investment in public buildings comes from the private sector through public/private partnerships;

   - GSA provides policy integrating workplace, workforce and IT issues;

   - GSA enables any Federal employee to work anywhere, anytime, with maximum capability;

   - GSA is the sole property disposal agent for the Federal government;

   - GSA is the primary supplier of applications service provider services (e.g. payroll, HR, accounting, etc.) to all Federal agencies.

- By 2010,

   - the need for new courtrooms is reduced through a programme of judicial courtroom sharing;

   - the rent paid and square footage needed by Federal agencies are reduced by 40 per cent;

(*continued*)

> **Table II.1.2   (continued)**
>
> o all Federal vehicles are powered by electricity or alternative (non-gasoline) fuels;
>
> o 75 per cent of Federal agencies have eliminated their shadow GSA organizations;
>
> o GSA is the management consultant for five cabinet agencies.

IMPLICATIONS, INSIGHTS

In 2000, GSA's mission statement read:

We provide policy leadership and expertly managed space, products, services and solutions, at the best value, to enable Federal employees to accomplish their missions.

A draft of GSA's 2002 mission statement reads:

We help Federal Agencies better serve the public by offering at best value, superior workplaces, expert solutions, acquisition services and management policies.

While the mission remains similar, the leadership agreed that the only certain thing about the future for GSA is that the current model of its behaviour cannot survive. Much of what GSA does is "supply chain" activity. At one level, GSA is about government operations, focusing on functions such as supply and acquisition. GSA operates today, for the most part, at this level. However, as the audacious goal exercise – based on scenarios – shows, GSA aspires to go beyond this transactional level to higher valued activity. Is GSA the future business manager for the Federal government? Can GSA bring the Federal government closer to the public? Can GSA become a "knowledge" broker instead of a broker of supplies and property?

There is every reason for optimism. GSA is actively engaged in working toward the goal to make GSA one of the best places to work in the USA, an audacious goal at a time when public service is not held in high regard. Furthermore, significant progress has been made to reformulate GSA's Internet presence as a customer-focused, high-value, knowledge site. Customer-focused market research has been introduced within the Office of Communications. GSA's court construction programme is now recognized as one of the most important contributors to public architecture in the country.

At GSA, futures research and scenario development have been used to teach us that times are *always* changing and to prepare us better to meet the challenges of such constant change in the public sector.

Consignia and scenario thinking

Consignia developed a view of the future and peopled it with three very different virtual reality characters to show the options and choices. These were used to develop new products and services. This case study has been contributed by Annette Hutchinson and Dr Maureen Gardiner of the Research and Consultancy Services Department in Consignia.

BACKGROUND

Consignia comprises three main brands: Post Office, Royal Mail and Parcelforce Worldwide. Consignia's ambition is to establish itself as one of a handful of key global distribution companies, trusted to connect every person, business and community in the UK and with the rest of the world in a way no other organization can.

Royal Mail delivers parcels and letters to all 27 million UK addresses, and its network of Post Office branches is by far the UK's biggest retail chain.

The global market for international letters and packages is worth some £20 billion and is forecast to grow to £57 billion by 2010. Royal Mail handles 1.5 billion items of international mail a year.

Consignia has joint ventures, acquisitions or stake holdings in eleven countries and the Business Mail Joint Venture consisting of TPG, Consignia and Singapore Post will create the world's largest business mailing partnership.

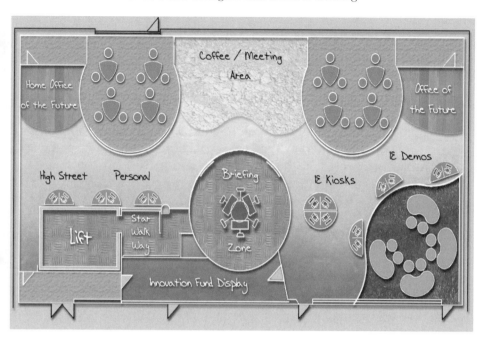

Figure II.2.1   The Innovation Lab.

FUTURES WORK IN CONSIGNIA

Research and Consultancy Services began combining social, technological and business projections to create scenario stories in August 2000. The catalyst was the introduction of a human resources specialist to a technology team at the time when an innovation centre (the Lab, see www.consignia.com/the lab) was being developed. This led to a unique combination of skills, perspectives and technical capability that resulted in a very different end product than would have been possible otherwise.

The Lab is a physical space that has been designed to stimulate and support creative and strategic problem solving facilitated by technology (Figure II.2.1). It also serves to open up participants to emerging and projected technology trends. It consists of four rooms with a wide range of collaborative software and a number of interactive demonstration areas that display future technologies and their potential impact. It is windowless with whiteboard walls throughout and intentionally sits in contrast to normal business environments.

Sessions at the Lab are facilitated by senior researchers and managers who use a range of creative and technology-supported techniques to increase the pace and range of solution development or problem exploration. Strategic workshops form part of the portfolio of events that the centre runs and these focus on long-term business planning, new product development and organizational change.

In August 2000, the challenge facing the facilitation team was how to support strategic planning so as to ensure that emerging trends were understood and absorbed as part of the planning or problem-solving process. A scenario-based approach was selected as having the potential to place planners in a future world that reflected these trends. The Lab environment meant that multimedia could be exploited extensively as a medium for presenting scenarios and supporting data. It could also enhance emotional acceptance of scenario possibilities.

SCENARIO DEVELOPMENT

The first stage of scenario development was extensive research into projected trends and thinking across a range of sources including commerce, academia and government.

The next stage was to identify major trends that appeared consistent across many credible sources and to use them to stimulate debate among internal researchers. This was done in workshop sessions at a Research Team away-day. The feedback from the researchers was of two types. First, issues to do with content (i.e. the projections and trends themselves that were added in or challenged due to the researchers knowledge base). Second, issues to do with understanding and translation (i.e. how well the form of material presentation conveyed understanding and insight).

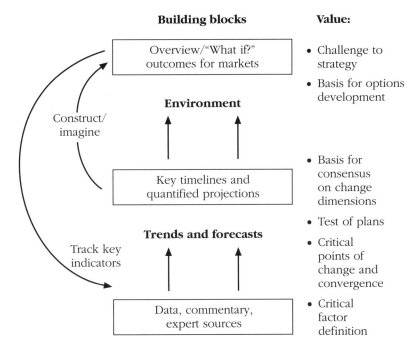

Figure II.2.2 Scenario structure.

The final stage was to construct the scenarios (Figure II.2.2). The approach that describes a number of polarized worlds representing extreme outcomes of "what if" analysis was rejected. The inherent improbabilities make it difficult for people to accept such scenarios as a substantive basis for planning.

Instead, a future environment was constructed that combined the major trends and forecasts in social factors, technology and markets. Within it, planners could see seeds of change, visible today, as they might play out with a sense of probability and scale. Against this common background, a number of demographic segments were selected and described as the archetypal consumers. The scenarios were built as the stories of their lives. This allowed full rein to "what if" projections, combined with more tangibly rooted trends and forecasts used to create the broad background to those lives. The benefits were several:

- maximizing acceptance of scenarios for the duration of the planning activities;

- consistency of focus, with a sustained understanding of the factors contributing to the scenarios;

- this structure – and the use of multimedia-enabled narrative, visual imagery and backing data variably combined and linked – allowed the scenario material to be used at several different levels;

- the logical separation of the trend-based environment and "what if" consumer outcomes made it easy to refresh and change aspects of the latter without wholesale reconstruction of the scenarios.

CONSIGNIA'S SCENARIO 2010

Using storytelling and narration, the scenario is exposed and described by means of three individual viewpoints (Figure II.2.3). These viewpoints epitomize some of the characteristics of particular customer segments that have been identified as important in the future and encourage focus and discussion on the drivers and differentiators of change. These three radically different but recognizable types of customer segment have great significance for Consignia because they represent a way of viewing customer segments and the extremes of the customer base. They can be linked to both corporate and unit level planning as well as providing a human face to the varied customers of Consignia.

Through narrative and visual imagery, a character describes the impact of technology, social, political and organizational trends. Based in the character's home environment as an anchor, working life, differences in values, and perspectives are explored.

The relationship with Consignia is also described against the background of each character's needs and projected technology trends. Products or services not yet available are deliberately

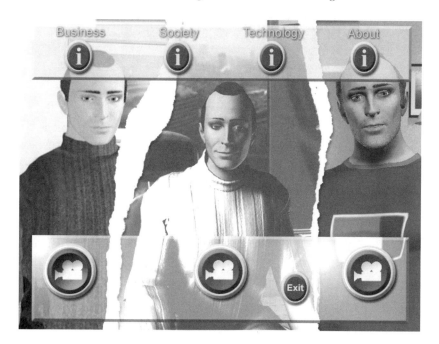

Figure II.2.3 Three characters and lifestyles.

raised as a stimulus for debate and innovation in the supporting session.

The characters and images were created using virtual reality techniques coupled with an actor's voice and are available on video/CD. The scenario is supported by a trend summary, projections, research source references and web links, all of which are on CD and suitable for group or individual review and interrogation.

Table II.2.1 summarizes the main differences between the scenarios/character viewpoints.

USING THE SCENARIO TOOL

The scenario tool has proven to be very flexible and is constantly being used in different ways. However, in the context of a standard

Table II.2.1	Three characters		
Character viewpoint	*Local Britain*	*Global citizen*	*Have-not*
Location	Semi-rural UK	City centre	Public housing
Key themes explored	Relationships, quality of life, transport, environment, mobile working, political environment, e-commerce	Small business service sector, security and health technology, immediacy of technology and business support, globalization of commerce	Employment trends, family support, social mobility, education

skeleton approach, which facilitators build on for strategic planning or new product development, the scenarios are usually used in the Lab. After a problem or output clarification exercise, participants view all or the relevant segment of the scenario to create a shared understanding of the future context they are planning for or the customer group or technical capability.

Then, collaborative software brainstorming, mind mapping and other creative techniques are used to capture and develop the key themes that need to be addressed. Participants are then invited to spend time drilling down through the information on the CD, which supports the scenario, to weight and inform their discussion on key issues to be addressed. This then allows solution or plan development to be shaped by what is projected and currently known as well as what may be possible but is as yet only projected as ideas in virtual reality.

Finally, where plans or products are being developed for national cross-customer deployment, the challenge session invites participants to test proposals from the different viewpoints shown.

THE RESULTS

Apart from the intended contribution of the project, there have been unexpected results from this approach:

- Quality of debate. The provision of a language and context for futures work frees participants to share, explore and challenge more openly. Frequently, participants have grasped with clarity some trend or insight that had eluded them. This has been true of all levels of participants across a range of topic areas. From boards discussing their customer base to researchers assessing breadth and depth of research, and operational units reviewing technological impact, the result has been the same. Participants have remarked on how much clearer this approach made the issues by summarizing masses of information into short stories of meaning.

- Desire for information. As a result of engaging with the information on the CD, managers often actively seek or commission targeted research into areas explored. In short, there are always lots of questions exploring the issues further and wanting to find out more. At a time when managerial time pressures are intense, this is a strong indicator of relevance and usefulness. It is also significant because it demonstrates how research knowledge can be made accessible and attractive to operational managers.

- Emotional transition. Individuals have remembered the quite complex interactions and characters and speak about them with insight after the event, even expressing their feelings about the characters. This level of engagement with the scenario creates the emotional acceptance necessary to develop strategy against that background. For instance, one group came to the Lab to review how technology would alter the size and functions of their team. This would normally be an emotionally charged topic, but on seeing the scenarios they actively planned their own restructuring. Why? Because they could grasp and make sense of what technology could do in the future, the changing demands of their customer base and how it freed them to redesign their way of working.

These results are achieved in sessions lasting half a day or more, although key players continue to seek additional information and continue to use the characters as reference points long after that. They work equally well with groups of all levels and functional backgrounds because they are about people in the future. They also help mixed level and function groups to mesh quickly by providing a common framework and focus.

EFFECTS OF USING THE SCENARIO

Some of the tests that we apply to the scenario are that:

- The quality of the scenario story and supporting data are recognized as relevant and credible by participants who relate immediately and personally to the substance of each scenario. There is not the challenge to credibility that can occur with more extreme types of scenario – rather, people see it as a credible, if challenging, projection of the future, not just an intellectual "workout" of remote possibilities.

- Individuals can see the seeds of the change now that will lead logically to the scenario presented. This means that individuals become equipped with an understanding of the drivers and relationships that allows them to plan and engage in debate over the key issues that Consignia needs to address. This is being confirmed constantly by participants who identify and contribute additional evidence for these seeds of change in market, technological and environmental factors. In this model, experts do not need constantly to tell line managers and planners what to remember as the devolution of understanding empowers them to act and plan independently and confidently. This achieves a fundamental objective for the Research Department: to share understanding rather than provide experts at every stage of a planning process simply because their expertise in incomprehensible.

- The use of the scenarios leads to a step change in the outcomes due to a shifting of focus into the future and an enrichment of the understanding and debate on issues to be addressed. This includes the extent and clarity of participants' collective memory of the scenario and their grasp of the key issues and relationships, which we have found to be stronger than any formal documentation process.

CONCLUSION

For us, the new step in this process is adding to the scenario tradition of storytelling an innovative combination of data access and virtual reality. This has captured the imagination and interest of participants, so increasing their grasp of the meaning behind the research and their confidence in thinking about the future.

Scenarios at the dti

This case study describes a public/private partnership in which ICL shared its experience in thinking about the future to work with the dti (The UK government's Department of Trade and Industry), to develop and manage a facility which both could use to facilitate their staff and customers in thinking about the impact of the future on their activities.

BACKGROUND

The dti is responsible for a range of regulatory and support activities for UK industry. It also funds a high proportion of university research and development. The future of many of these functions will change in the global marketplace. The dti was also concerned about the effect of European Commission plans, of regional parliaments in the UK, of the changing face of industry and the growth of the service and knowledge economies.

ICL had been a core supplier of IT to dti for many years, and had developed an understanding of the Information Society through its earlier scenario work (Ringland, 1997). Two other companies partnered with ICL and the dti: Silicon Graphics, a supplier of graphics servers and workstations used as standard for virtual reality, and Trimension, which designs and builds virtual reality "theatres".

THE CHALLENGE

Understanding how the role of government is changing requires imagination and vision, to see how people may behave differently and want different standards of service from governments and the private sector. Futurists have this vision; the question for the dti was how to communicate it.

The changes that government expects over the next decade are many, complex and interrelated. Though many stem from technological discontinuities, the effect is likely to be different by industry, by country, by age group, by access. How can these be integrated for a government audience?

Enthusiasts are often "one topic" enthusiasts. Thinking about the future with an enthusiast is frustrating – the focus will be technology, the environment or demography. The vocabulary will be full of certainties, the outcomes very positive or very dire. The world is complicated, and government strategists had found that many audiences reacted badly to "the world will be like this" predictions – because they can see many reasons why it may be otherwise.

SCENARIOS TO COMMUNICATE POSSIBLE FUTURES

John Reynolds, then Director of the Futures Unit at the dti, decided to use scenarios. A team of civil servants and consultants developed a set of three scenarios for the dti in 2015. The axes of uncertainty were:

- individualistic values/restricted knowledge sharing vs. shared values and knowledge inclusion;

- global cohesion vs. global fragmentation.

Within this framework, very different future challenges could be seen for government. The scenarios were initially described with slide sets and time lines and used widely in training sessions. But for decision makers, a different approach was taken.

A number of different techniques are valuable for describing scenarios to decision makers. These range from descriptive names and elevator speeches (30-second descriptions, suitable for starting and finishing between floors) to the use of plays and newspaper headlines to explore the global, local or human dimensions of a scenario. A sign of success for scenarios communicated in this way is a response of: "and I can see that for my life or business, this scenario would look like . . .".

LEARNING FROM ICL'S PREVIOUS EXPERIENCE

Meanwhile, ICL had developed an approach called "futurefocus" for helping its customers think about the opportunities to enhance their business through IT. Initially focused on retailers, it took a "day in the life" approach to tracking a family's use of information technology to organize themselves, their work and leisure activities. The technology used was real, and every aspect was in use in at least one organization, though no organization would be using all of it together. So, for instance, an intelligent "Frig" was used to send electronic mail – an electronic panel added to the front of an ordinary domestic refrigerator was used as a bulletin board or terminal for electronic mail. Shopping ordered in the morning from the workplace desktop was delivered to the workplace and collected by the shopper from the company's security desk in the afternoon. Data mining was used to explore a customer base and its interests.

The total effect was to communicate effectively to organizations with interests far wider than retailers such as those in government, manufacturing, travel, media and financial services. The costs of the "visits" are significant in terms of skilled manpower, utilization of space and refreshing the site and equipment, and design overheads. So, they need to be designed to maximize usefulness to the visitors and to the hosts.

ICL also found that one of the ways to improve the utility was to design in the right amount of time, during a visit, for the customer management team to exchange ideas about what they had seen and to discuss the impact on their organization. We borrowed from the experience of the Post Office's Innovation Unit, who had designed a Creativity Lab (see Section II.2). By using a combination of unorthodox surroundings, skilled facilitation, and software to aid brainstorming and convergence, they had encouraged groups of people to create their own solutions and move their business forward.

ICL had experimented with virtual reality as a method of giving people a glimpse of the future, for instance technology that was "not yet here", and found that the ensuing discussions prompted real thinking about business opportunities (Ringland, 2000).

FUTUREFOCUS@DTI

John Reynolds of the dti and the author (then at ICL) realized that the two organizations together could create a better experience for our respective constituencies than either could separately. We decided to design a facility for team events that would follow a sequence of experiences (Figure II.3.1):

- A virtual reality theatre, to give an immersion experience in the scenarios. This has a long curved screen 8 feet high by 30 feet long, and seats up to 15 people with good immersion.

- An "interactive society" area, giving hands-on access to devices that are precursors of those seen in the future, to allow people to get a feel for the timescale of the arrival of technology.

- A Creativity Lab, to allow the team to discuss their ideas arising from what they have seen and understood, and to develop an action plan. This has walls that can be written on, laptops accessing brainstorming software (see Section III.5), and is delib-erately built with curved irregular walls and variable lighting. This has proven amazingly effective at providing a problem-resolution environment for cross-departmental issues.

This was based at the dti's headquarters. ICL, with partners SGI and Trimension, supplied the equipment, physical design and project management to implement the facility, and usage is shared.

USING SCENARIOS AT FUTUREFOCUS@DTI

Futurefocus@dti has been extensively used by the dti and its private-sector partners, encountering rave reviews.

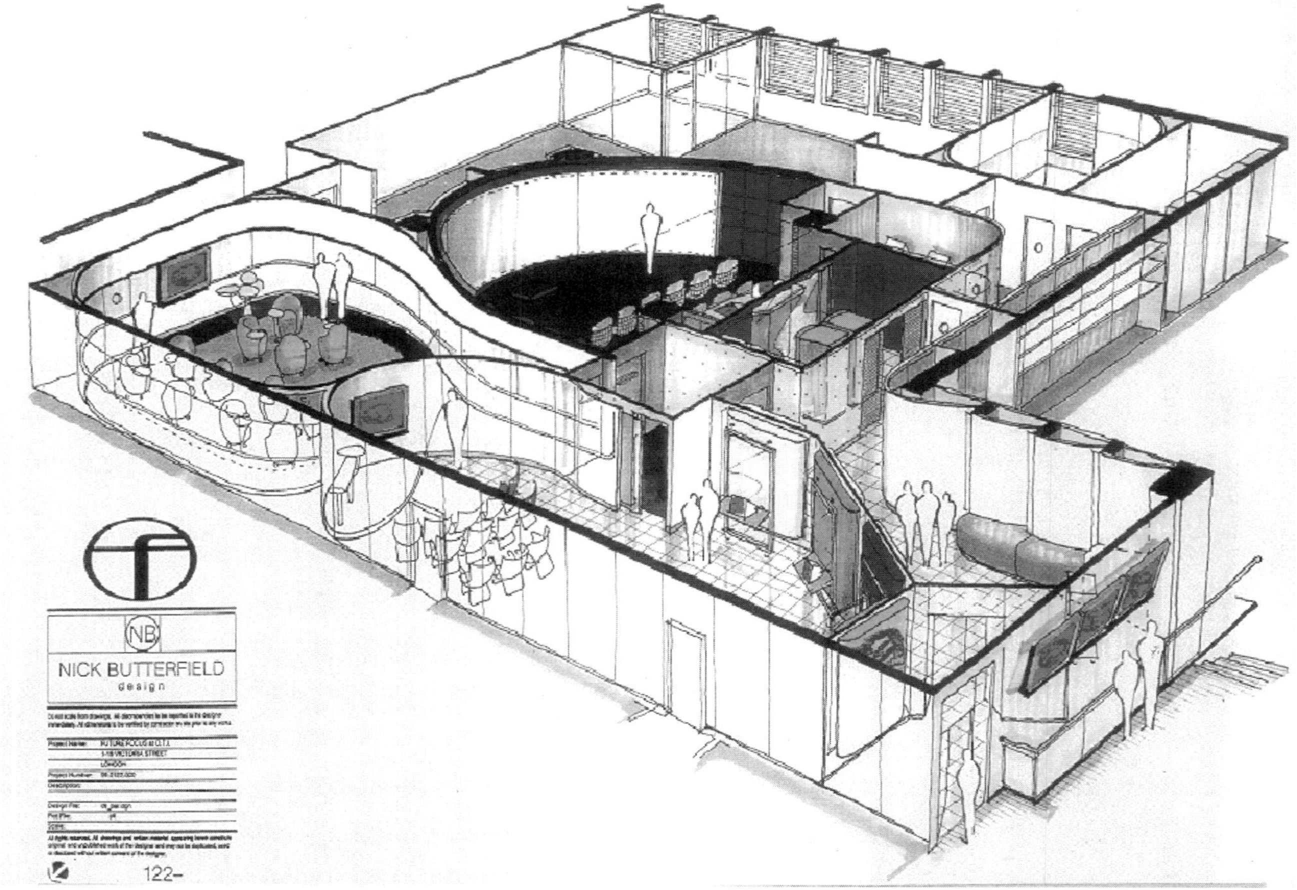

Figure II.3.1 Layout of futurefocus@dti (reproduced by permission of Nick Butterfield).

108

In the public sector, one typical event hosted by the DTI was for a government department that was considering how to widen citizen participation in the democratic process, as part of the social inclusion agenda. Within futurefocus@dti, the department assembled senior policy makers and advisers. Moving through the three different environments, the group considered the economic and social environment under the three scenarios. For more detail, see Yapp (2001).

The day-long event consisted of three stages:

- In the immersive theatre, the group saw vignettes of examples of social inclusion and exclusion under the three scenarios up to 10 years ahead: Who will be the excluded and who the included under each scenario? This helped them to understand the drivers of change and consider the causes of social fragmentation. The theatre is also equipped with data modelling tools that allow them to explore demographic changes interactively and interrogate the model with varying assumptions.

- The "interactive society" area helped the group to consider what is technically possible today, to encourage participation through making it easier to vote. The group considered voting via the Internet with a range of devices and discussed security implications.

- The creativity lab helped the group think about the access to technology of different demographic groups:
  - Is access via digital TV the most fruitful?
  - Could all community centres be put on a national network?
  - The elderly may be slow to take up new technology: How can they be supported?

The group brainstormed options and voted on the most promising for development and implementation of a plan in the department.

In the private sector, ICL, SGI and Trimension have designed events to share the future with their staff and customers. The author was surprised and pleased to hear a group from an advertising agency excitedly discussing the conceptual breakthroughs in understanding that they had made in the facility, while she was strap-hanging on the London Underground.

LESSONS LEARNED

- A well-designed environment can unlock previously intractable tensions and allow a group to reach agreements or innovations they had not expected.

- Using scenario visualization in a theatre environment with frequent pauses to discuss decision points and strategy issues, which brings a freshness that allows the group to get back to first principles.

- A half-day event based on the existing scenarios, presented in this way, can achieve agreed and actionable plans.

Scenario planning goes to Rome

Since 1989, Global Business Network (GBN) has been engaged in a series of related scenario learning projects with the De La Salle Christian Brothers, a Catholic religious congregation (also known as the Institute of the Brothers of the Christian Schools or simply "the Institute"). This case study focuses on the introduction of global scenarios for the future of the Institute to the year 2015 at its 43rd General Chapter in Rome in May 2000. In GBN's 14 years of experience with scenario planning, this case stands out for two main reasons: it is the first time in our experience that scenario planning has been used at the highest level of governance for a major religious congregation, and it is perhaps the best example to date of the use of scenario planning to foster strategic conversation across a wide diversity of cultural, ethnic and national back-grounds within one organization. This case study was written by Chris Ertel and is reproduced with his permission.

BACKGROUND

The first Lasallian school was founded in 1679 by Jean-Baptiste De La Salle, an affluent Frenchman who felt a calling to devote his life and personal wealth to address the poverty, exclusion and ignorance he saw among French youth at the time. By providing free, faith-based education, De La Salle and his small group of followers believed they could transform the lives not only of dis-tressed youth but of themselves as well. The Lasallian mission remains essentially the same today: to provide a human and Christian education to the young, especially the poor. Today, the

Institute is the second-largest teaching congregation within the Catholic tradition (after the Jesuits), with more than 6,000 Brothers operating over 1,000 schools and other works in more than 80 countries, serving over 850,000 people every year. In this work, the Brothers are joined by over 60,000 "lay partners" who carry out the bulk of the work of the mission. By contrast, at the beginning of the 20th century the Brothers were responsible for virtually all the work of the mission.

Closely associated with the challenge of the ageing and declining number of Brothers is the issue of the transfer of leadership toward lay partners upon whom the future of the mission will depend. Indeed, the order faces three main choices: (1) find a way to increase the number of new vocations to the Brotherhood; (2) consolidate the works of the Institute as the number of Brothers declines; or (3) gradually transfer leadership to lay partners, while still safeguarding the spirituality, history and values of the congregation. While all of these possibilities are discussed, it is generally (though not universally) accepted that the third option is the most likely future path. How and when this gradual transfer of leadership might occur is a matter of great debate – one that is complicated by the tremendous diversity of local conditions across the international Institute.

THE CHARACTERISTICS OF THE INSTITUTE

Scenario planning has been used in a wide range of organizations all over the world, including most major industries as well as in many government and non-profit settings. Still, in several respects, this engagement is sharply distinct from more "typical" cases, including:

- *A values-driven mission with lifelong commitment and a communal lifestyle.* While many organizations claim to be "values driven", few of them rely on the willingness of individuals to devote their entire lives to these values, even to the point of foregoing traditional families. Brothers agree to live in small spiritual communities that function as virtual families. As such, the dynamic of relationships among key actors is far more complex than in other kinds of organization and may result in a reluctance to address areas of conflict directly.

- *An extremely decentralized organizational structure.* While the Institute's highest level of governance (the General Council) is based in Rome, the structure of the organization affords a high level of regional and local autonomy in determining how the work of the mission should be adapted to suit local conditions. Most important decisions about organizational strategy, including major investments and leadership, are made at the local and regional level.

- *An extremely high level of diversity of cultures, languages and local conditions.* While many organizations talk about "going global" – usually starting from a main headquarters location rooted firmly in one place and culture – the De La Salle Brothers have been a truly transnational organization for decades. Brothers work in (and themselves come from) such diverse settings as Brazil, Singapore, Nigeria, India, Spain, the USA, Japan, Poland, and many more places. In some places, like Malaysia, the Brothers provide for teaching from the Koran as well as from the Bible.

- *An unusually long time perspective.* Unlike most organizations, there is frequent appeal to the distant past experience of the organization within the Institute. In our workshops, it was not uncommon for participants to refer to events that took place 50 or 100 or even more than 300 years ago. For example, when talking about pressing challenges, it was not unusual for participants to recall that the Institute had been through bad decades in the past, so that a rough next 10 or 20 years might not be much to worry about!

DEVELOPING THE SCENARIOS

Leading up to the 43rd General Chapter in Rome, the GBN team engaged in three scenario projects on distinct (yet related) focal

Figure II.4.1 The scenario matrix (reproduced by permission of Chris Ertel).

issues of critical importance to the organization: (1) models of membership and association for the relative roles of Brothers and lay partners in service to the mission; (2) how to better connect the works of the Brothers with the rich and the poor around the world; and (3) the future leadership needs and appropriate models for the Institute. Representatives from 11 countries participated in a total of 6 workshops, including a total of 30 Brothers, 17 lay partners and 8 external participants invited for their expertise in relevant topic areas.

After the completion of all three projects, the core team integrated the main lessons learned from each of them. The framework selected was a matrix (Figure II.4.1) with two axes that represent two critical uncertainties in the external environment that will affect the global Lasallian mission over the next 15 years:

- Will economic trends lead towards an uplifting of economic conditions in the developing world, or will the trend towards increasing inequality between rich and poor areas in the world accelerate?

• Will social, political and spiritual trends be towards more or less cultural acceptance of, and support for, the Lasallian mission in the years to come?

It is important to note that the scenario matrix can be seen as representing two things at the same time: (1) a "snapshot" of present reality across the global Lasallian community; and (2) a "scenario space" or a moving image of directions in which the future might turn in different places.

THE SCENARIOS

Looking at this matrix as a "snapshot" of the present, we can see that there are four very different present realities that can be seen as existing in the world.

Wealthy areas that are unsupportive of the Lasallian mission (upper left quadrant)
Today, such areas include Japan and Holland: affluent non-Christian or secular societies where participation in the formal Catholic Church is low and/or falling, and where general activity in private philanthropy is weak (often because the state is expected to provide social benefits). In such areas, the greatest challenges for the Institute relate to overcoming the general indifference in society to the work of the mission.

Poor areas that are unsupportive of the Lasallian mission (lower left quadrant)
Today, such areas include Cuba, Vietnam, and Pakistan: places where local leaders often show outright hostility to Christianity and the work of the Brothers. In such areas, the greatest challenges are often just surviving and providing help in areas where the Brothers are unwanted or in some cases even forbidden from teaching.

Poor areas that are supportive of the Lasallian mission (lower right quadrant)

Today, such areas include the Philippines, Mexico and Poland. These are the "feel good" areas where the work of the mission is both desperately needed and generally supported by society. In such areas, the greatest challenges relate mostly to leveraging enough resources to meet the tremendous demand that exists for the work of the mission.

Wealthy areas that are supportive of the Lasallian mission (upper right quadrant)

Today, such areas include the USA, Australia and much of Europe: wealthy areas where, generally, there exists significant resources and support in society for the work of the mission. In such areas, however, the greatest challenges relate to realizing a level of organizational excellence that allows the Institute to compete effectively in a highly developed marketplace for providing quality, values-based education.

EVOLUTION FOR EACH SCENARIO

Thus, looking at our matrix as a "snapshot" of the present, we can see that each quadrant represents a very different reality with different assets and challenges. Next, looking at our matrix as a "scenario space", we can see that there are also possible stories to describe how and why each one of these realities might grow more quickly than the other three over the next 15 years. Below is a very brief outline of the four scenarios.

Sowing faith in an elitist world (upper left quadrant)

This scenario describes a world in which a growing number of people are living affluent, middle-class lifestyles with a strong emphasis on personal choice and individual self-expression. Interest in personal spirituality is on the rise, but people are turning away from traditional religious institutions. The De La Salle Brothers are confronted with a difficult decision between bending to the increasingly secular times or taking a more counter-cultural position. (Examples of places moving in this direction today include Ireland and Italy.)

Heroism amidst hostility (lower left quadrant)
In this scenario, a severe global economic downturn leads nations and cultures to curl in upon themselves, defending traditions and attacking those with promises of progress or unfamiliar religious beliefs. The potential for values-based education is strong, but the resources are lacking. Where the Lasallian mission thrives, it is due mainly to inspiring acts of heroism under difficult situations. (Examples of places moving in this direction today include Colombia and the Congo.)

Faith perseveres in adversity (lower right quadrant)
The climate in many developing nations – especially non-Christian nations in Asia and Africa – becomes friendlier to the Lasallian mission, creating tremendous opportunities. Governments in most developing countries feel the desperate need to improve educational systems, and most are open to supporting schools of different faiths. However, resources are scarce, requiring that the Institute find creative, new ways to reach out to more people for support. (Examples of places moving in this direction today include India and Peru.)

The challenge of success (upper right quadrant)
This story describes a world that is largely uplifting but in which the Institute has a hard time keeping up with the pace of progress. Education becomes the number-one cause of the new millennium, and many nations succeed in dramatically reducing illiteracy and poverty. (There are few obvious examples of places moving in this direction today, but it is possible that several countries in Asia and/ or Latin America might experience this kind of take-off in the coming decade.)

Before the final scenario matrix and detailed narratives (which ranged from six to nine pages each) were taken to the General Chapter, they were tested on a "road show" before meetings of Institute leaders in three regions: Latin America, Asia, and North America.

Introducing Scenario Planning at the 43rd General Chapter in Rome

The core team approached the 43rd General Chapter with a fair amount of trepidation. Would the 129 Chapter delegates from more than 50 countries find the scenarios understandable and useful? Would they engage with the material or just find it a curiosity?

The interaction with the scenario work took place over two days at the beginning of the six-week-long General Chapter. Three respected Brothers explained the scenario framework and narratives, and facilitated the strategic conversations. On the first day, conversations were conducted in three separate breakout groups – one for each of the three official languages of the Institute: English, French and Spanish. On the second day, the scenario conversation expanded to a plenary session with all delegates, with simultaneous translation delivered by headphones in all three languages. Prior to the discussions, all delegates received a detailed report with the scenario narratives and background documentation.

The design of the interaction was greatly enhanced by the use of a rich visual interface that served as a physical representation of the strategic conversation. The scenario matrix was created in huge poster form, complete with a collage of visual images consistent with each different reality and scenario narrative. This poster was then deployed as an interactive board game, in which each delegate was invited to locate his present situation and likely future trajectory (based on current trends).

Interacting with the scenarios

The interaction of the delegates with the scenarios took place in the following steps:

1. Each participant was given a card, colour-coded by region, with his name and district on it, and was asked to tape the card to a position on the matrix that best represented his present reality.

2. A conversation was held about the challenges to be found in each quadrant of the matrix. All delegates found it easy to situate themselves in one quadrant or another, and those who were within the same quadrants generally agreed that they faced

118

similar sorts of challenges. The scenario framework thus usefully reduced the complexity of local conditions in a way that had never been done before.

3. The scenario narratives were summarized by discussion leaders. It was explained that, even though a delegate might situate himself in one quadrant today, he could find himself in a completely different quadrant in the near future and facing very different challenges.

4. Each delegate was then given a red adhesive arrow to attach to their name card, to indicate the direction that they believed their local area was heading in the future (i.e. which of the four scenarios seemed to be unfolding before them).

5. Finally, delegates engaged in a broader conversation to interpret together the pattern of arrows indicating that different future scenarios did in fact appear to be playing out in different places at the same time.

The conversation that resulted from this process was lively and productive. Delegates realized how their different local realities differed from each other within the context of a shared framework. Many delegates moved the position of their cards in reaction to the positioning (and reasoning) of other delegates. The conversation that followed reflected a deeper appreciation for the interrelation of the various parts of the Institute and the importance of understanding better the challenges of others – in part because you never know when they could become your own!

ASSESSING THE IMPACT WITHIN THE LARGER ENGAGEMENT

For the remaining six weeks of the General Chapter, the scenario poster was displayed prominently as a reminder of the conversation that took place. But what impact did the scenarios have on the work of the General Chapter? For an inside view, Brother Armin

Luistro, a Delegate and Visitor (Director) of the District of the Philippines, offered his perspective:

It is obvious that the delegates to the General Chapter were not familiar with scenario planning. However, I observed that most who chose to attend our sessions were keenly interested in the new insights that were presented as a result of the global perspective that the scenarios provided. It was clear that the general directions of the Institute will have to take into consideration two important variables that can change reality radically depending on world developments. I am convinced that the recognition that there are at least four scenarios for the future and that the Institute may actually be located in four different worlds awakened in the participants the fact that while we could strive to work in synergy, we may not necessarily do things uniformly. From the point of view of the organizational structure of the Institute, the visual representation of where each sector might be located with reference to the four quadrants provided the participants with a view of possible new groupings in the Institute where sectors are brought closer to those others whose contexts are similar to theirs even if they are very different in language and culture or geographically distant. Most groupings in the Institute are based on geographical location, language or cultural links.

Consistent with this observation, General Chapter delegates ultimately passed a number of resolutions that addressed key issues raised by the scenario work – especially those related to more aggressive fund-raising efforts and greater inclusion of lay partners. At the same time, however, Brother Armin notes that scenario planning did not fully succeed in encouraging delegates to rise above more parochial agendas:

When one looks at the resolutions passed during the 43rd General Chapter, one begins to realize that not too many delegates have a feel of what is happening worldwide and thus, they support strategies and programmes which may be helpful for their own sector or perhaps their own region but which on the whole may not be a wise move for the Institute.

In Brother Armin's view, the scenario perspective was an important step in helping to broaden the thinking of Institute leaders, but that the process will take a great deal more time and effort – especially at the local level, where most of the real decisions about the future of the organization are made. While the General Chapter engagement was challenging, its most important impact in the long run will probably be that it set the stage for much more local-level work, where results can be more tangible.

The larger engagement with the De La Salle Christian Brothers is ongoing, so that no final word on the effectiveness of these efforts is possible. There is evidence that participants in scenario planning activities have embraced the need for more long-term and externally oriented thinking on an ongoing basis. However, it is far too soon to tell if these efforts will enable the organization as a whole to meet its aging challenge in time. To be sure, deep culture change takes time; fortunately, so does the ageing process!

LESSONS LEARNED

The team has identified five simple lessons for scenario planning practitioners that were learned from our intervention at the 43rd General Chapter:

1. *The importance of a simple framework, especially when facilitating communication across a wide range of cultures, languages and local situations.* When encountering scenario planning for the first time, many people can find this way of thinking both counter-intuitive and abstract. In this case, the high level of cultural and linguistic diversity added to the communications challenge considerably. The ability to summarize the narratives within a simple framework (i.e. a 2×2 matrix) was key to engaging participants in meaningful strategic conversation.

2. *The power of using an interactive visual display to represent the conversation over time.* In this case, the matrix poster with name

121

cards and arrows allowed participants to "watch" their conversation evolve as their understanding of each other's different realities grew.

3. *The utility of enabling the client to take the lead role in creating the strategic conversation, especially in delicate situations where business consultants are not usually included.* If GBN had not engaged highly respected Brothers to lead the scenario discussions, it is hard to imagine that they would have received the kind of positive reception that they did.

4. *The need to draw upon the organization's own language, history and internal narrative in portraying alternate futures.* In the course of testing the scenario work at the pre-Chapter "road show", the core team found that using established language and narratives from the organizational culture was critical to gaining acceptance and engagement.

5. *The necessity of a multifaceted approach to culture change that includes top–down and grass roots efforts simultaneously, especially within a highly decentralized organization. Finally, one lesson from the larger engagement is that any longer term attempt at deep culture change must engage the organization at different levels. In this case, the greatest impacts have been at the local level, while the groundwork of high-level exposure at the General Chapter has been key to establishing the credibility of the scenario work. Any attempt to reach one level without addressing the other would clearly not have been as successful.*

Finally, we will leave the final word on this work to the primary client for this work, Brother David Brennan, the Visitor (Director) of the District of San Francisco:

Looking back on the scenario planning work undertaken by the Brothers, I found the process to be invaluable for engaging a myriad of agendas, cultural perspectives and strategic priorities facing us as a worldwide community. The process and content helped us understand the critical uncertainties and possible scenarios in different realities in the world. The scenarios generated a useful strategic conversation in three languages at our worldwide gathering in Rome. These customized scenarios challenged our mental maps and enabled many to understand and respond to the signs of the times. It also provided a powerful platform for making important decisions while engendering a sense of urgency. In the District of San Francisco, we used it to wind-tunnel and strengthen our existing action plan and to accelerate key strategies and priorities (such as a much more ambitious fund-raising effort) that were revealed by the scenarios and strategic option generation.

The author would like to acknowledge the extended core team for their work in this project, as well as for their thoughtful comments on this section. At GBN, this includes: Michael Mulcahy, Jay Ogilvy, Kees van der Heijden and Joe McCrossen. At the De La Salle Institute, this includes Brother David Brennan, Brother Stanislaus Campbell, Brother Armin Luistro, Brother Miguel Campos, Brother Paul McAuley, Gery Short and Tom Brady.

Decision making in the public sector

This section by Tom Ling is based on his experience of developing and working with scenarios and futures studies. He concludes that, for a number of reasons, futures work fails to make an impact on public sector policy, and suggests some of the reasons. The author's views are personal and do not reflect the official opinion of his employer. He is grateful to Philip Hadridge for many useful discussions.

BACKGROUND

The author has described the development and use of scenarios in, for instance, the health service in a number of papers based on the *Madingley* scenarios (Ling, 1999a, b) for health care.

The scenarios have led to a range of projects, mostly related to the health sector. Topics have included:

- *The impact of developments in new human genetics on health services.* The *Madingley* scenarios were used to inform future service models for delivering health services during a Department of Health workshop on the future organization of genetics services, held in September 2000. The author was closely involved in designing and delivering, between 1999 and 2000, the Nuffield Trust's scenario project on the impact of new human genetics on health services.

- *Managing uncertainty in Siberian children's services and in health care services in the Moscow region.* The author led a three-day scenario planning workshop on service configuration with managers of childrens' health services in Irkutsk, Siberia held in November 2000. He was similarly involved in a project in Moscow in the spring of 2001.

During this time, the author has had the chance to observe at first hand how scenarios have been built and subsequently used in the UK and other public sectors. He perceives that the link between futures work or scenarios thinking, on the one hand, and the effect on policy and planning, on the other hand, is at the best opaque in the UK public sector and at worst non-existent. He suggests some reasons for this and makes proposals for increasing the effectiveness of the input to policy and planning.

WHY IS GOVERNMENT INTERESTED IN FUTURES?

The differences between public sector planning 30 years ago and now is typically explained in terms of globalization, new technology and heightened interconnectedness. This is linked to the weakening of bureaucracies, the hollowing out of the nation state and a breakdown of trust in traditional sources of authority. Culturally, we are said to be entering a world, which is both eternal and ephemeral, where nothing is permanent except the permanence of change. This is not the place to assess whether this belief that the world had changed so dramatically is justified. There are some important ways in which the future has become less controllable and these ways matter. It may be that the extent of these ways has often been exaggerated – especially by those selling tools to manage this uncertainty. After all, when selling a new product, it helps if the consumer believes that the old product is useless. There are also pressures leading the academic community to exaggerate the dimensions of change (see Clarke, 2000 for a critique of this claim). Despite the need for more enthusiastic advocates to tone down a little, it is also true that significant areas of public policy involve interventions into complex systems with limited instruments while there are a prevalence of powerful drivers over which public authorities have little control. For example, the author is required to develop policies concerning the future configuration of genetic services with limited knowledge about the scientific, cultural, social and regulatory context which will exist in even five years time. And doing nothing is not an option. One expression of this in the UK is that it is a key objective of the *Modernising Government* White Paper (Cabinet Office, 1999 and http://www.cabinet-office.gov.uk).

FUTURES AND SCENARIOS ACTIVITIES

Recent developments in futures thinking meet a real and perceived need among policy makers in the public sector. There is now a Strategic Futures Group within the Cabinet Office and the Cabinet Office has promoted interest in the tools and techniques of futures thinking, including:

- a paper on "the future and how to think about it" (PIU, 2000a);

- a paper benchmarking strategic futures work (PIU, 2000b);

- studies of methodologies (PIU, 2001a);

- a meta-analysis of published material on drivers and trends (PIU, 2001b) identified 50 studies as being sufficiently relevant to inform British public policy.

In addition, the Foresight programme, begun under the Conservative Government in 1993, has continued alongside significant futures-oriented work within many government departments, in particular the Department of Health and the Defence Evaluation and Research Agency. Other organizations such as the Royal Institute of International Affairs (Chatham House, 1996), the Nuffield Trust (Dargie, 2000; Zimmern and Cook, 2000), the Open University Business School and projects such as the Tomorrow Project (Moynagh and Worsley, 2000) have all responded to a perceived need for better forward-looking thinking. Other "futurist" influences on the public sector include:

- Shell's "Global Scenarios 1998–2020" (see Table III.1.1, p. 142);

- CIA's "Global Trends 2015" (see Table III.1.1, p. 142);

- European Commission Future Studies Unit's "Scenarios Europe 2010" (European Commission 1999).

So, there is widespread evidence of futures thinking in and around the British policy-making community.

GOVERNMENT AND RISK

In addition to such formal futures-studies activity in the public sector, "the future" has entered into policy makers' thinking through a heightened emphasis on risk management. All policy makers are expected to think about the risks associated with a policy and how these might best be managed. For example, the Private Finance Initiative and, more recently, Public Private Partnerships both depend on the capacity to generate an account of the future in which private sector involvement might be said to provide better value for money in general and risk management in particular. In turn, this requires the future to be modelled in order to support decisions. Other tools helping to manage risks include the creation of narratives about the future through simulations and soft systems modelling.

The "core studies" identified in the meta-analysis produced for the PIU are held to be particularly relevant for policy makers in Britain. These all reveal a particular concern with uncertainty. They are all more concerned with identifying the range of possible futures rather than with quantifying the likelihood that any particular future will happen. However, the fact that the Cabinet Office has identified these scenarios as significant and useful for policy makers is in itself revealing. The mechanistic economic models favoured in the 1960s aimed to provide policy makers with certainty. Policy makers today are being offered more flexible tools for handling uncertainty.

FUTURES THINKING AND PUBLIC POLICY MAKING IN THE UK

The question is, how has this been used and could it be used more successfully? Trying to answer this is fraught with practical and methodological difficulties:

- Practical problems arise because so many policy decisions are taken behind closed doors, and it is hard to gauge the impact of scenario work on this.

- The methodological problems arise because policy making is a complex response to more or less explicitly articulated developments. Even the participants themselves may not fully understand how and why decisions were reached. Worse still, policy makers often disagree about what happened.

- Although the *Modernising Government* White Paper places great emphasis on policy making being future focused, it remains unclear which version of the future policy makers are expected to focus on.

- There is now a growing body of literature on policy transfer and policy learning from overseas and the author can trace clear linkages from ministers or advisors spending time looking at how a policy works elsewhere to applying the lessons at home. There is no parallel body of work on futures thinking. This, of course, is partly because it is more difficult to visit the future than to organize a study trip to another country.

TWO HURDLES TO BASING POLICY ON FUTURES

The first impression is that the UK's constitutional arrangements and lines of accountability focus decision-making power in the hands of

Ministers who, in turn, are accountable to Parliament. This constitutional accountability is reinforced by media that are intolerant of politicians should they openly acknowledge that the future is uncertain. Neither Parliament nor the press appears yet ready for a Minister, far less a Prime Minister, who argues that the future is complex and that policies will be designed on this basis. Inevitably, the reality is different from the dignified fiction that ministers alone make decisions. Decisions are taken at a variety of levels and are more mutually interdependent than hierarchically driven. But acknowledging this and creating a policy-making culture based on this is hard to achieve within existing constitutional constraints.

Second, for policy makers, futures work shares the same frustrating quality as policy-related academic work: it rarely points unequivocally to one course of action. If "what counts is what works" is part of the credo of the new policy maker, it will be frustrating to acknowledge that he cannot always clarify what works. Expressing uncertainty is seen to be politically the weak and administratively untidy. In response to such lack of certainty, the hard-wiring of British public policy making becomes apparent.

POLICY TO TACKLE CURRENT PROBLEMS

Where the purpose is clear, as in times of war, the policy-making process is remarkably effective. The finest hours of Churchill, Thatcher and Blair have all been in times of conflict. However, where the ethics are contested, the science uncertain, the evidence flaky and public opinion ill-formed (e.g. as with GMOs), the system slips into near-paralysis punctuated by orgies of poorly informed action (BSE, foot and mouth, etc.). In these circumstances, the more inclusive and deliberative style of government favoured in, for example, the Netherlands lends itself to more successful outcomes, which enjoy greater legitimacy and are more informed by available evidence (see the case study on Rotterdam and Arnhem, Section I.2)

SCENARIO THINKING AND PUBLIC POLICY MAKING IN THE UK

In this environment, the implications of scenario thinking, emphasizing the importance of a variety of strategic capacities to cope with a range of possible future circumstances, clashes with the existing institutional architecture.

If formal obligations constrain and centralize decision taking, so too do the preferred cultural instincts of Whitehall and the British governing classes.

Most scenario work has been commissioned by and written for senior decision makers; any insights are not shared throughout the organization and they are not used to construct an inclusive style of decision making. Nor have they mostly been concerned with promoting organizational flexibility (but see the case study on the dti, Section II.3).

For many experienced strategists, the ability to make decisions based on a range of possible futures, to maintain flexibility, is a key role for scenarios. This requires an understanding of the possible environments by staff at all levels. The author's impression is not of a governing class seeking to be inclusive through its futures thinking but, on the contrary, of a class anxious to sequester knowledge and to construct 'the future' as the official version.

CONCLUSIONS

The impact of futures thinking and scenario planning on public policy in the UK is limited by the existing institutional architecture and cultural context in which policy makers operate. This works badly for many of the emerging problems facing the UK, although its capacity to galvanize a nation behind a shared project with clear objectives should not be dismissed.

Since the author believes that the UK would be strengthened by a wider impact of futures and scenario thinking on policy, he suggests that the next steps should be:

- to gain policy-maker recognition of what sort of issues benefit most from being explored by scenario thinking;

- to explore what changes to the institutional arrangements might facilitate this sort of work; and

- to take some pilot projects forward in a visible and metricated manner.

Lessons learned

The lessons learned as a result of the projects described in the case studies in Part II relate to both scenario use in particular and the more general lessons relating to long-term or strategic thinking and action in the public sector.

CREATING THE SCENARIOS

- *The need to draw upon the organization's own language, history and internal narrative in portraying alternate futures.* The core team found that using established language and narratives from the organizational culture was critical to gaining acceptance and engagement (Rome, Consignia).

- The quality of the scenario story and supporting data are important to allow participants to recognize the substance as relevant and credible (Consignia).

- *The importance of a simple framework, especially when facilitating communication across a wide range of cultures, languages and local situations.* When encountering scenario planning for the first time, many people can find this way of thinking both counter-intuitive and abstract. In The Christian Brothers case, the high level of cultural and linguistic diversity added to the communications challenge. The ability to summarize the narratives within a simple framework (i.e. a 2×2 matrix) was key to engaging participants in meaningful strategic conversation (Rome, GSA).

COMMUNICATION OF THE SCENARIOS

- Effort put into creating an environment for promoting innovation and FUD-free discussion works. A well-designed environment can unlock previously intractable tensions and allow a group to reach agreements or innovations they had not expected (dti, Consignia).

- Using scenario visualization in a theatre environment with frequent pauses to discuss decision points and strategy issues, "Should DTI support regional regeneration of a particular type under this scenario?" brings a freshness, allowing the group to get back to first principles. A half-day event based on the existing scenarios, presented in this way, can achieve agreed and actionable plans (dti).

- *The utility of finding natural leaders to take the lead role in creating the strategic conversation, especially in delicate situations where business consultants are not usually included.* Finding highly respected natural leaders to lead the scenario discussions increases positive reception (Rome).

- *The power of using an interactive visual display to represent the conversation over time.* In the case of Christian Brothers, the matrix poster with name cards and arrows allowed participants to "watch" their conversation evolve as their understanding of each other's different realities grew.

OUTCOMES

- Individuals can see the seeds of the change now that will lead logically to the scenario presented. This means that individuals become equipped with an understanding of the drivers and relationships that allows them to plan and engage in debate over the key issues (Consignia).

- Experts do not need to constantly tell line managers and planners what to remember as the devolution of understanding empowers them to act and plan independently and confidently (Consignia).

- The use of the scenarios leads to a step change in the outcomes due to a shifting of focus into the future and an enrichment of the understanding and debate on issues to be addressed. This includes the extent and clarity of participants' collective memory of the scenario and their grasp of the key issues and relationships, which we have found to be stronger than any formal documentation process (Consignia).

- Any longer term attempt at deep culture change must engage the organization at different levels (Rome).

- An approach to culture change must include top–down and grass roots efforts simultaneously, especially within a highly decentralized organization. Action in meeting challenges is often at a local or regional level (Rome, GSA).

- Futures or visionary work in the public sector by employees may not be readily endorsed by politicians, since politicians do not necessarily have a corresponding time span of interest (GSA, Decision making).

- Scenarios create visions of the future which can be used to develop new products, markets or business models (Consignia, GSA, Rome).

- Practical problems arise because so many policy decisions in the public sector are taken behind closed doors, and it is hard to gauge the impact of scenario work on this (Decision making).

- The methodological problems arise because policy making is a complex response to more or less explicitly articulated developments. Even the participants themselves may not fully understand how and why decisions were reached. Worse still, policy makers often disagree about what happened (Decision making).

PART III

MAKING SCENARIOS WORK

SUMMARY

This part contains a number of checklists and dos and don'ts aimed at facilitating the successful use of scenarios by managers.

Section III.1 is "The environment for scenario thinking", covering factors such as timing, the human dimension and whether the aims of the manager can be accomplished by using an existing scenario set.

Section III.2 is a guide to the overall process, and Section III.3 is a guide to the practicalities of getting started. If it reads like a project management guide, it is!

Section III.4 is one of the key sections about deciding the question – often the outcome of initial interviews. Section III.5 covers more practical detail such as interviews and workshops, and the role of tools.

Section III.6 describes the mechanics of scenario creation, discusses "how many scenarios" need to be created and gives guidelines for developing the storyline.

Section III.7 covers the crucial "scenarios to plans" stage, and Section III.8 discusses linking scenarios into the organization: techniques for communication, and aligning with the organization's research and intelligence operations.

Section III.9 summarizes the main points and lessons learned, and concludes that "Scenarios are part of strategic management: their use rather than their existence is the key to success".

The environment for scenario thinking

A scenarios project will be successful if people make decisions that are influenced by it. Some of the factors that increase the chances of success are listed, as are some sources of publicly available scenarios that may be an alternative to in-house development. Scenario thinking can be a part of an organization's armoury in a number of situations. This section pulls out some generally applicable pointers to a suitable environment. The subsections "Engaging stakeholders" and "Adapting the scenarios" are reproduced from Berkhout (2001) with the permission of Crown Copyright.

WHY SCENARIOS?

Scenarios are now accepted as a management tool. Where is their use best focused?

- The use of scenarios in developing public policy through engagement with the stakeholders has been very successful. By clarifying believable possible futures, the community can address the issues (as in the case studies in Part I).

- Scenarios provide an environment for creating a shared context and language inside the organization. This is important in an environment where specialists or people from different cultures or departments need to contribute to solving a shared problem and implementing the solution (as in the Consignia and GSA case studies, Sections II.2 and II.1, respectively).

- Scenarios are indicated where the force of the external world requires senior managers to think "outside in" in times of structural change (as in the dti and Christian Brothers case studies, Sections II.3 and II.4, respectively).

Many organizations additionally flag other benefits of scenarios; for example:

- Creating a common language; many scenario thinkers today believe that the most significant outcomes of scenario projects are a sense of vision, allowing the organization to pull together to implement it.

- Creating a cadre of people with strategic thinking capability and a network across the organization.

- Allowing teams to cooperate on issues outside the operational time frame, with consequent reduction in tensions from current roles. By focusing on a horizon, defensive attitudes to current responsibilities are less relevant. Would you expect to be doing the same job in 10 years' time?

BEFORE YOU START

Engaging stakeholders
The key challenge of the scenario planning process is to engage stakeholders inside and outside the organization. It can only be successful in promoting creative and unconventional thinking if the process is based on engagement and trustful relations. However, the usefulness of the scenario planning method is sometimes contested. Thinking 10, 20 or more years ahead is not routine for most organizations and can seem difficult or meaningless. Scenarios are also criticized because the underlying assumptions can rarely be validated and are to some extent a matter of judgement. Scientists often express concerns about using an inherently subjective framework in the context of research. Practitioners sometimes feel that a scenario exercise does not generate sufficient tangible outcomes:

- Engaging stakeholders requires, first of all, clarity about the aims and limitations of the approach. Scenarios are not aiming to predict the future, or not even to identify the most likely future. Instead, they map out a "possibility space" to inform the decisions of the present. The scenarios method is based on sub-jective choices (as in fact is any other approach to explore uncertain futures), but, unlike other tools, it allows stakeholders to discuss and challenge these judgements.

- If participants are to be convinced of the importance of their contribution, the aim of the scenario planning process needs to be well defined and clear indications need to be given as to how the results will feed into decision making.

The time needs to be right
The outcomes of the project should be ready to feed into the organization's thinking when the organization is asking for direc-tions into the future: the scenarios for South Africa were created to influence the political process leading to the seminal elections in 1994. In other projects, timing may depend on the availability of participants.

It is not a good time:

- when the organization is very unstable at decision-making levels;
- if the results will be available just after a major strategic planning round has completed and set for implementation;
- if the organization is in panic mode.

It is a good time:

- Just after a new appointment at strategic levels.
- If timing allows the scenario outputs to be input to a strategic planning round.
- If the organization is facing specific challenges such as:

○ rethinking the role of a department of central government in response to policy changes and changes in the constituency;

○ changes in demographics require new thinking on the use of school buildings and teachers;

○ organizations facing new challenges from the private sector in health, education, transport, media or communications.

Get the organizational framework straight
Who is the client?

• Does he or she have access to budget and is the first stage underpinned by clarity of purpose?

• What is the reporting structure?

• If consultants are used, are they working *for* the project team or *with* the project team?

• Are there opponents to the project – beware of hidden agendas?

• Identifying the first manager to work with in applying the scenarios is a good preliminary step; in fact, a preliminary project focused on his or her needs may be a useful introduction.

Scope and deliverables
Be sure to understand what is needed and when:

• Is the scope of the study, coupled with the deliverables, timescale and support (e.g. research staff), clear?

• The people who will do the work should be identified early on: secondees from around the organization are ideal, and outside consultants are a great help in giving the project status and in facilitating the process.

- Deciding the timescale for your scenarios. For example, "Scenarios for Scotland in 2010" for a project completed in 1999 is a significant choice of date in that the new Scottish Parliament would have been in place 10 years by then, posing the questions: What does Scotland want the Parliament to achieve? What does Scotland want to be?

DO YOU NEED TO CREATE SCENARIOS?

An important early decision is whether to create specific scenarios for the organization or to base the scenario thinking around existing scenarios. The case study in "Foresight Futures 2001" (Section I.8) describes the use of environmental scenarios with multiple constituencies. Using pre-existing scenarios as a basis for work in an organization – or country – makes a lot of sense under some circumstances; for example:

- where the external environment is a dominant factor (e.g. the economy), use scenarios that are based on extensive desk research on economic futures;

- where the intention is to introduce scenario thinking to a group of people, without the investment in time to research and build specific scenarios;

- where many of the same considerations apply to all departments in a company, and where a business unit wants to explore alternative futures.

Which to choose and where to find them
The sources in Table III.1.1 are all in the public domain. Section III.5 gives an agenda for a workshop using existing scenarios.

Table III.1.1	Sources of scenarios		
Sources of scenarios	**Timescale**	**Topic**	**Website or ISBN**
Richard Baldock	2008	Organizations	0-471-98462-0
Chatham House Forum	2015	Economy of the industrialized world	www.chforum.org
CIA	2015	Global trends	www.cia.gov/cia/ publications/ globaltrends2015
Coates and Jarrett	2025	US and global society	www.coatesandjarrett.com
UK Foresight	2020	Environmental	www.foresight.gov.uk
Glen Peters	2015	Customers	0-273-62417-2
John L. Peterson	2015	Security	1-878-72985-9
Gill Ringland	2005	Information and communications technology	0-471-97790-X
ScMI	2010	Global manufacturing	www.scmi.de
Shell	2050	Energy needs, choices and possibilities	www.shell.com
Singapore	2004	Trade, technology and tribe	www.gov.sg
World Business Council for Sustainable Development	2050	Sustainable development	www.wbcsd.ch
WIRED	2020	Commercial life	www.wired.com/wired/ scenarios

ADAPTING SCENARIOS

The scenarios in Table III.1.1 can provide a generic framework but they may not contain enough detail on many sectors or policy domains. To elaborate scenarios for any given domain of interest requires:

- identification of key drivers in the sector (e.g. international markets, social preferences, regional planning);

- an assessment of the links between drivers and relevant sectoral trends;

- specialist knowledge of the sector.

Producing four scenario elaborations can be time consuming, with diminishing returns according to effort. One alternative is to choose a smaller number of scenarios for in-depth analysis (say two or three scenarios). Some studies have chosen to look at diametrically opposed scenarios (e.g. *world markets* and *local stewardship*, as in "Foresight Futures 2001", Section I.8). However, equal effort should be put in to scenario elaboration during a first phase to avoid the risk of narrowing down the thinking too early.

Effort devoted to the development of indicators will vary between studies. Indicators may be illustrative of the storylines, or they may be outputs of the scenario planning exercise that are used in further analysis (planning, options appraisal or scientific modelling).

Simple scenarios are more accessible to non-specialist audiences. However, in longer or more intensive scenario planning exercises, users may want to introduce surprises (see Section III.6) and additional factors. There are several ways of achieving this:

- Two scenarios can be combined (e.g. one for the UK level and one for the international level). This process needs to be selective because there are many possible combinations. The choices made will depend on what is realistic and relevant for the study in question. For example, a scenario exercise on the UK manufacturing industry could examine the effects of an international *world market* scenario combined with a *national enterprise* scenario, as in Section I.8.

- Another approach would be to introduce a third dimension (driver of change) relevant to the sector: high or low technology scenarios have been tried in a number of exercises including the Special Report on Emissions Scenarios (SRES) for the Intergovernmental Panel on Climate Change (IPCC, 2000). In this case, the effects of different assumptions about the adoption of energy technologies in the future was analysed in detail for one of four socio-economic scenarios.

- If the original set of scenarios is thought to oversimplify trends, it is possible to add a second round of scenario elaboration encouraging participants to think about feedback mechanisms. This allows learning processes to be taken into account. One option would be to organize this round of the evaluation as a "game-playing" simulation (see Section III.8).

The stages of a project

The 12 stages of a scenarios project are described and illustrated, from identifying the focal issue or decision through decisions and/ or publicizing the scenarios. A good overall guide to the first part of the process, developing the scenarios, is to be found in Peter Schwartz's The Art of the Long View *(Schwartz, 1997). The sub-section "Getting the process right" is reproduced from Berkhout (2001) with permission of Crown Copyright.*

GETTING THE PROCESS RIGHT

Maximizing the learning benefits of scenario planning exercises requires close attention to process. Careful planning and structuring of the scenario elaboration, synthesis and evaluation stages of scenario planning are needed. The details of the process will be tailored to the needs and resources available in each case. The process needs to accommodate integration of a diversity of viewpoints and technical expertise, producing an iterative process combining creative, participative workshops and work carried out by individuals or in small groups to synthesize and elaborate scenarios. Realism is needed about the time and resources needed to complete an exercise – this tends to be underestimated. Time is needed in the participative aspects of elaboration and in the process of making sense of the results. Finally, stakeholders need to be involved in the elaboration of scenarios at an early stage.

THE 12 STEPS

Checklist for developing scenarios

This checklist extends that given in Schwartz (1997).

Step 1.   Identify focal issue or decision

Step 2.   Key forces in the local environment

Step 3.   Driving forces

Step 4.   Rank by importance and uncertainty

Step 5.   Selecting the scenario logics

Step 6.   Fleshing out the scenarios

Step 7.   Implications for strategy

Step 8.   Selection of leading indicators and signposts

Step 9.   Feed the scenarios back to those consulted

Step 10. Discuss the strategic options

Step 11. Agree the implementation plan

Step 12. Publicize the scenarios.

STEP 1: IDENTIFY FOCAL ISSUE OR DECISION

The focal issue or decision may be obvious. In the US General Services Agency, it was "*What is the effect of e-commerce?*"

The focal issue may determine the scope (timescale, geography), or the organization may have specified the scope in advance (e.g. Scotland in 2010), when the focal issue was "What role would Parliament play and what vision would it have for Scotland?"

In other cases, it needs to be teased out. For instance, in

Consignia, interviews with a number of external and internal people led to the question: *"How are customers for Royal Mail changing?"*

STEP 2: KEY FORCES IN THE LOCAL ENVIRONMENT

Forces in the local environment will influence the success or failure of decisions about the key question. These will include customers, suppliers, competitors and internal groups. What will the decision makers want to know before they decide?

As an example, in the case of Consignia, new postal services were being announced, and the work force was taking industrial action over a range of issues. How could different services for new customers be made attractive to the workforce?

Listing these key factors is Step 2; they are sometimes referred to as microeconomic forces, and are often the factors elicited by interviews or issue workshops (see Section III.5).

STEP 3: DRIVING FORCES

Forces in the macroenvironment that will affect the key factors are known as the driving forces. These will include the PEST set (political, economic, social, technological), but may be extended by particular forces such as demographics or public opinion.

Research is usually needed to find the relevant drivers, and to understand their trends and possible or likely breaks in trends. Examples might be in demographics, the effect of immigration on numbers and education level of people in London, where instead of the forecast about a declining and ageing population a growing young population was uncovered in the *London in 2020* project (Ringland, 1998).

STEP 4: RANK BY IMPORTANCE AND UNCERTAINTY

The key factors or microeconomic forces, and the driving or macroeconomic forces, are ranked on the basis of two criteria: importance to the decision identified and uncertainty.

The point, as Peter Schwartz says (Schwartz, 1992), "is to identify the two or three factors that are most important and most uncertain." These will provide the main differentiators of the scenarios, but there may be two stages before the two or three are identified.

First, some macroforces may best be felt and measured through their effect on key factors, and so are subsumed in these.

Second, do not lose sight of the fact that important but predictable forces may be more significant to the decision than the uncertainties. Demographics may, for instance, be a major force compared with political uncertainties.

STEP 5: SELECTING THE SCENARIO LOGICS

The logics are the axes of uncertainty arising from the ranking. Two or three driving forces or key factors (usually driving forces) are used to create a visual map of the scenarios. The aim is to end up with a few scenarios that will be perceptively different to the decision makers.

So, for instance, if one driving force is "social values", the poles of this axis might be "individually dominated" and the other "community/consensus dominated". If the other driving force was globalization, the axis might go from "regional/local decision making" to "global forces dominate". Four scenarios could then be:

- individual/local;

- individual/global;

- community/local;

- community/global.

This raw positioning will become more complex as other factors in the scenario are added, a storyline developed and a timeline added.

STEP 6: FLESHING OUT THE SCENARIOS

Once the logics are fixed, return to the lists of driving forces and key factors identified above. Sometimes, the logics are reasonably correlated with the driving forces. For instance, in the example above, a strong regulatory regime could exist in different forms according to the local/global orientation, but would not be found under a highly individually oriented society. Other factors may be constant across the emerging scenarios; for instance, technology developments might be a common factor whereas technology adoption could be argued to be higher under individually-oriented societies, except where government initiatives exist.

The forces and factors need to be turned into a narrative, answering questions such as:

- How would we get from here to there?

- What events would need to happen for this to come true?

- What sort of people would characterize the scenario?

STEP 7: IMPLICATIONS

Now, the test of it all. How does the question to be decided look under the different scenarios? Do we come to the same answer under all of the scenarios? Does the same strategy fit whichever scenario plays out? For instance:

- in "Four scenarios for public education in Seattle" (Section I.1), the implications for community involvement and success are significantly different for each scenario, and a visionary scenario was included to provide a blueprint for action;

- the development of the Christian Brothers (Section II.4) would necessarily be different under each scenario.

STEP 8: SELECTION OF LEADING INDICATORS AND SIGNPOSTS

It is important to be able to track which scenario is nearest to history as it unfolds. The way to do this is by identifying some events or economic indicators that would only be found as part of one of the scenarios. It is best if these can be indicators which are tracked anyway by the competitive intelligence unit, and be unambiguous (e.g. named people, companies or levels of statistical indicators). It is also important that the escalation route is clear so that the unit that obscures the trigger event knows what to do about it.

The workshop described in "Tackling big issues in 24 hours" (Section I.5) was one of the consequences of tracking an early indicator from scenarios. The indicator for was the funding of EU research and development programmes for "The Information Society". The programme was refused funding by the European Parliament. We found out why: it was techno-ignorance among many politicians. So we started on a campaign to bring politicians, government and the private and voluntary sectors together to understand the dynamics of "The Information Society" and its differences from the industrial society (Ringland, 1997).

STEP 9: FEED THE SCENARIOS BACK TO THOSE CONSULTED

The emphasis is on finding the right method of feedback: packaging, naming and storyline are, as in any communication exercise, vital. One-on-one feedback is preferable to groups, and applying it to a decision that the interviewee had mentioned or has by now started to face is the most effective way.

In public policy work, the format used in Rotterdam and Arnhem (Section I.2) was via a building with rooms for each scenario, and in Arnhem additionally via postcards for visitors to fill in to give their preferences.

In Consignia and the dti (Sections II.2 and II.3, respectively), an innovative interactive environment was designed specifically to feed the scenarios back.

STEP 10: GENERATE AND DISCUSS THE OPTIONS

Section III.7 describes the method of generating and deciding on options, by creating a matrix of a complete set of options against the scenarios, and grading them from very positive through to very negative. So, for instance, in an e-commerce scenario, investing in electronic channels to market would be positive, whereas the same option could be negative in a scenario focusing on traditional outlets.

The choice of options will depend on organizational capability. Most will need to follow options that span realistic scenarios, and watch for early indicators on others.

STEP 11: AGREE THE IMPLEMENTATION PLAN

There will usually be a project owner who can agree the implementation plan. This will need to cover:

- early indicators, responsibility and escalation route;

- implementation of agreed strategies and options;

- publication of/publicity for the scenarios.

STEP 12: PUBLICIZE THE SCENARIOS

When scenarios are intended to influence public opinion or to facilitate discussion within an organization, the same questions arise as in a marketing capaign:

- What are the target audiences?

- Who are the decision makers and who is an influencer?

- Who will benefit and who will lose out under each scenario? How can their needs be met?

- What channel can be used to reach the target audiences?

- What events are critical in time sequence?

- What are the success criteria (i.e. when do we stop!)?

Getting started

This section prompts us to ensure that the project is well-thought out. It discusses communicating the aims, scope and timescale of the project to the budget holder, setting up the team and connecting it into the organization.

HOW TO GET STARTED?

Start with a definite event: a presentation, a brief or a lunch. What to cover should include:

- the aims of the project, scope and timescale;

- the team and its reporting structure.

PRE-PLANNING CHECKLIST

Like any successful project, scenario planning needs clarity at the outset.

Aims of the project, scope and timescale
See Section III.1 on the aims and scope.

Timescale
- One-day workshops can enable a management team to plan their actions based on existing scenarios. This is easier if there are only

two scenarios (if this is the only workshop planned, introduce with the brief on the aims of the workshop and project).

- Scenario workshops taking two days can build outline scenarios that bring out the main issues in the competitive environment and initiate wide-ranging action.

- In two weeks, an experienced team with a good database of environmental analysis and intelligence can create scenarios and use them with a management team to develop new strategies.

- Six months is a more normal elapsed time to produce well-rounded scenarios and an action plan that takes the need to organize input and feedback into account, as well as to develop strategy.

- Even if the use of scenarios is seen by the team as ongoing, each stage (e.g. production of the first scenarios) will need to be defined.

- When are the deliverables required (e.g. aligned to the planning cycle, availability of key people).

What are the deliverables?

What form of output is required and to whom? The list in Section III.8 is a guide to the manager on the type of scenario presentations for onward communication. There will of course also be the need for regular milestones and reporting during the project.

THE TEAM AND ORGANIZATION

Who is the client?

This was discussed in Section III.1.

Team

- Scenarios can be developed by one person, but they are improved by access to experienced "friends".

- A range of backgrounds is useful, including a non-public sector background.

- A core team of three is frequently chosen, and they should share interviews and workshop facilitation, preferably working in pairs. The key roles are:

  ○ team leader to set the overall aims and schedule who, with a network including the planners and the Board, is responsible to the project owner for delivery;

  ○ organization "old hand" with a wide network of people across, but especially at the front end of, the organization (e.g. project managers, call-centre managers);

  ○ visionary and/or outsider who is willing to pose difficult questions and comparisons.

- Other skills:

  ○ access to an experienced scenario planner, who may be from outside the organization, either as a consultant or taking over the delivery responsibility part of the team leader role;

  ○ access to a good communicator to help test output, who may well be external, and provide a neutral communication role rather than being expert in the domain or organization;

  ○ access to libraries or web data sources – see "Deciding the question" (Section III.4) for a discussion on the role of research, and "Linking scenarios into the organization" (Section III.8) on the role of intelligence.

ORGANIZATION

But, even more importantly, you will need links into the organization: not everything will be appropriate for all organizations or for all projects:

- The senior decision makers. How will you keep them informed, interact on the ideas as they emerge or get early wins through implementing plans based on the scenarios?:

  ○ Advisory Board;

  ○ progress reports to/meetings with CEO;

  ○ work directly with the Board in workshop mode.

- The organization's middle managers and old hands:

  ○ electronic links, Intranet;

  ○ find the opinion leaders for and against changes;

  ○ a low-key workshop early on with a business unit to develop all or part of the scenarios.

- The organization and industry's movers and shakers, visionaries:

  ○ make them allies early on;

  ○ informally discuss the ideas with them and quote them liberally;

  ○ a workshop early on with a team built round one or more visionary.

Linking the project into the organization

- Via head of planning or senior sponsor:

  ○ head of planning if a centrally driven project;

  ○ senior sponsor if particular to a business unit.

- Advisory Board or "champions":

  ○ geography and diaries may make email and online discussion forums more effective than an Advisory Board;

  ○ champions should be forward-looking and need not be senior, but need to be role models and not frustrated with the organization.

- Mixture of workshops or interviews to get input:

  - two-day workshops give good momentum, more ideas, generate interest;

  - interviews by phone less good than face to face;

  - workshops can tackle aspects of the problem space with experts;

  - workshops can tackle "what is the question" with a mix of attendees;

  - getting the Board for two days is not usually an option.

- Chief Executive or equivalent – briefed if not involved through Advisory Board:

  - an early interviewee;

  - get suggestions for champions and interviewees/workshop attendees.

- Who to interview:

  - 100 interviews are too many, 10 are too few;

  - need for a mix of line and staff, insiders and outsiders;

  - people outside the organization who have provocative views;

  - the list will increase as you explore the questions.

- Whether to seek wider input:

  - electronic via email or Intranet, good safety belt;

  - if using volunteers for workshops, get those with time to spare rather than those with significant roles or views;

  - research and business intelligence undertaken by the organization in the context of the scenarios helps widen awareness of the project (see Section III.8).

- Feedback after the scenarios are in place:

  ○ management group (in person if possible) and discuss applications of the scenarios to strategy at the same session;

  ○ planning group or planners across the organization (in person if possible) and discuss default scenarios in the "official future";

  ○ interviewees (by email or phone) unless specifically requested to visit;

  ○ workshop attendees (similarly by email or phone).

- Communication of scenarios:

  ○ team member in person usually needed;

  ○ slide set and/or video;

  ○ storyline description, with implications for organization spelled out;

  ○ possibly, a brochure;

  ○ possibly, briefing via Intranet or for public policy using a website set up for the purpose; and

  ○ virtual or real images as in the case studies.

- First use of scenarios:

  ○ solving a problem or developing a strategy;

  ○ dry run the methodology to use in advance with the team;

  ○ also plan for issues workshops with several management teams or groups of stakeholders.

What is the best mixture of central and dispersed activities?

- The team needs to be able to meet for the sort of interactions that are less effective electronically.

- Interactive bulletin boards or email discussion groups can replace or augment some interviews and workshops.

- Secondees from across the organization are very valuable, as are workshops held outside the home base.

Deciding the question

This section outlines the role of research and interviews in deciding the focal question, and provides sample checklists for exposing the driving forces for some of the main applications of scenarios in business.

INTERVIEWS, WORKSHOPS AND RESEARCH

Scenarios explore the possible answers to questions about the future. They are most useful when the scenarios directly explore questions of concern to the organization. Interviews, either with individuals or groups, are usually used to create a list of factors that will affect the world and to identify the big questions. Workshops may be used to explore the factors (e.g. to get depth of understanding on a specialist area). And research will usually be needed to tie down data and known or predicted factors.

RESEARCH

Research will often involve two stages. At the first stage, research concentrates on ideas. This will identify some of the major forces affecting the organization.

Then, it will usually be necessary to tie data and known or predicted factors down. However, research should always be done in the context of a specific set of questions: the gathering of data is enormously facilitated by the web, making quantitative data and qualitative data easily available. It is easy to drown in data and miss the crucial areas: teams of two are better at maintaining focus than a solitary worker. Data sources which are widely used across a range of industries and countries include:

- OECD data on developed countries;

- Economist Intelligence Unit reports;

- forecasts such as in Pearson (1998);

- industry- or field-specific analyst and think-tank reports (e.g. on health, financial services, technology);

- government statistics on demographics and lifestyles.

However, be careful of using extrapolations based on historic data: for instance, the official projections were that the population of London would decrease and age from 1990 to 2000 as it had done over previous decades; but changes in immigration, mobility of students and increases in education and media industries in London meant that by 2000 the population was younger and higher than in 1990.

SEVEN QUESTIONS FOR THE FUTURE

Most people have an understanding of how their world works, but often it is not voiced or shared. This questioning technique works on the basis that people know a great deal, but do not always know what they know.

These questions (Table III.4.1) are to trigger thinking: the key is to understand the person's perceptions and unlock their strategic thinking. The technique could be used on an organization, a company, an industry or even a country. It should be done for a specific area of interest and over a relevant timescale. They are widely used and originate in Shell.

Table III.4.1　The vital issues (the Oracle)

1. *Critical issues.* Would you identify what you see as the critical issues for the future? (When the conversation slows, continue with the comment: Suppose I had full foreknowledge of the outcome as a genuine clairvoyant, what else would you wish to know?)

2. *A favourable outcome.* If things went well, being optimistic but realistic, talk about what you would see as a desirable outcome.

3. *An unfavourable outcome.* As the converse, if things went wrong, what factors would you worry about?

4. *Where culture will need to change.* Looking at internal systems, how might these need to be changed to help bring about the desired outcome?

5. *Lessons from past successes and failures.* Looking back, what would you identify as the significant events which have produced the current situation?

6. *Decisions, which have to be faced.* Looking forward, what would you see as the priority actions which should be carried out soon?

7. *If you were responsible (the "Epitaph" question).* If all constraints were removed and you could direct what is done, what more would you wish to include?

TAILORING THE QUESTIONS

Depending on the nature of the problem to be addressed, later interviews and issues workshops may tackle different aspects and need different preparation. However, it is likely that three common areas of uncertainty will arise:

- technology: rate of change or adoption;

- globalization vs. regional/localization;

- community values vs. individual values.

A country, city or region is considering its future

The questions may be ongoing or prompted by changes such as devolution. The common danger is in focusing too much on the change and not enough on the ongoing environment; for example, the common three, plus:

- economic strengths and weaknesses of the country, city or region;

- public amenities and transport;

- financial constraints (e.g. changing tax base);

- opportunities with new industries through technology; and

- specific change (e.g. new government).

For these scenarios, the extent of consultation and of dissemination are as important as the scenarios themselves: the aim is to produce a set of decisions over the next years which are more informed than would otherwise be the case.

The boundary between the public and private sector is changing

Use the list of questions in Table III.4.1; however, the team should have done some preliminary thinking on:

- problems facing the organization as functions that move across the boundary;

- new sources of competition;

- success criteria of existing partnerships.

Workshops will give more creative thinking than interviews in this environment. The key questions and opportunities will be difficult to tease out and internal issues will take a lot of time to be set aside:

SWOTs of existing and potential competition and partners are good diagnostic tools once the scenarios are in place.

One pitfall to avoid is that the planners and staff groups may have different sets of assumptions from the views on the ground. Using existing scenarios, provoke discussion about likely scenarios and the implications for the organization by separately running:

- workshops for planners or custodians of the official future;

- workshops for units at the sharp end facing change.

One way of doing this is by fleshing out the official future from planning guidelines, and describing it as a scenario, then using an externally defined scenario and comparing the differences on, for example, the common three areas of uncertainty.

Political and economic change creating fear, uncertainty and doubt with associated staff morale problems
The interviews and workshops should focus on:

- capturing the areas of fear, uncertainty and doubt;

- creating scenarios that tackle different views of how these areas play out;

- looping back to individuals early on with outlines to ensure the real issues are being discussed.

Scenarios for the environment
The important considerations for these tend to be:

- economy and technology;

- governance;

- ecology and demography;

- community values vs. individual values.

So far, most of the scenarios for the environment have been focused on professionals in the corporate or government sectors (see the case studies in Part I).

DECIDING "THE QUESTION" FROM A SET OF INTERVIEWS AND WORKSHOPS

- Define a set of terms that cover, for example, the three common areas of uncertainty.

- Analyse the interviews using these headings and then add other categories defined as broadly as possible:

  o location of key new facilities (as in Rotterdam, Section I.2);

  o desired future (as in Bueren, Scotland and Seattle, Sections I.3, I.4 and I.1, respectively);

  o changing boundaries;

  o staff issues;

  o infrastructure.

The differences in views on the topics will flavour the scenarios:

- Identify the focal issue or key decision to be made:

  o the issue may be a single one (as in Rotterdam) or a cluster of related issues (as in Seattle);

  o the issue may be external but the decision is about what to do in the organization, as in the case studies in Part II.

The decision outcome will probably be different under different scenarios.

NORMATIVE OR VISIONARY SCENARIOS

In scenarios intended to engage the public, as in the case studies in Part I, a visionary scenario often emerges, and is used by the administration to direct effort to achieving this.

Scenarios are also often used to drive out desired futures for organizations in the public sector, as in the US General Services Agency example in Section II.1.

Interviews and workshops

This section provides guidelines and sample agendas for interviews and workshops, and discusses some tools to assist and improve the process. It notes that while interviews have been the basis of much scenario fact and issue gathering, workshops/focus groups and email/ bulletin boards are increasingly being used to fit with the pace of the time, used in addition to or replacing interviews. This section has been greatly improved by thoughts from a presentation given by Adrian Davies of St Andrews Management Institute, UK.

PRACTICAL TIPS ON THE INTERVIEW PROCESS

• Consider the number of interviews carefully. Aim to get a range of views from different parts of the organization, different countries, a mixture of senior board members or in the public sector, establishment figures and identified high flyers or thinkers. Try to include people from outside the organization. The volume of information generated from these interviews made the analysis very time consuming: allow at least two hours per interview for analysis. Remember that the interview schedule will need to be extended as the project progresses.

• Plan how best to feed the "internal" issues back. Much of the information concerns internal organization and culture. This needs to be packaged and fed into the relevant areas in the organization, so that interviewees know that these ideas are not lost.

- Confidentiality. To get the best ideas and thoughts from people, it is advisable to stress that individual comments will not be attributed. Some people are nervous about taping of the interviews, and ask for assurances on the security of storage of the tapes and the control of identification of the source of each script. A scribe is useful if tapes are not being used, so that eye contact and concentration is maintained. Interviews are written up (but not usually sent to the respondent), and are kept securely by the team.

- Setting the scene. Advise the respondents before the interview that no pre-work is required. Ideally, it is best to get people away from their desk and in a different environment, so they can think creatively. In practice, the interview will be slotted into a busy senior managers schedule. In order to get people in the mood to think about the future and express their ideas, the interview needs to be relaxed and enjoyable. Most people find they jump around from one topic to another. It is best to try and encourage them, rather than make the interview seem like a set of questions with right or wrong answers.

- Set the time horizon clearly (e.g. 10 years or 20 years) and the scope (e.g. the future of information technology or the future of Scotland), and define the objectives of the exercise and anticipated output. Discuss any concerns with the timescale or scope that the interviewee might have.

- Interviews should only be constrained by the schedule of the respondent – up to say two hours. Interviewers should avoid leading questions, using, instead, the seven questions in Table III.4.1, for instance.

- At the end of the interview, the interviewer should ask whether the respondent has anything to add, and whether they had found the interview useful themselves. Leave the interviewee good time to think about both of these. Describe to the interviewee what will happen next and what will be visible to him/her.

- Plan group interviews outside the offices to encourage divergent thinking. Group interviews are not focus groups, the participants set the agenda. They are useful in, for example, country scenarios to bring in large numbers of disparate views. They usually result in consensus views, but using Groupware software (see Section III.5) can help ideas rather than personalities to dominate.

- Group and individual interviews are merged to create a "trial agenda" around a few major themes. This often reveals gaps in the evidence leading to desk research or additional interviews. The trial agenda becomes "the agenda" when a complete set is collected and collated in a formal document under change control.

ISSUES WORKSHOPS

After about 10 interviews, a few factors or issues are likely to emerge as the list of major questions to be addressed by the scenarios. All members of the team must sign them off before any issues workshops are held. The list should be fed back to the CEO or client, as should any unwelcome items in the evidence.

One way of testing that these are the right issues, how they interact with each other and how they may change over the timescale of the scenarios, is to enlist the help of a group of challenging people (interviewees and outsiders) to create an outline structure. The issues should be considered in the order:

- External world:
  - issues already raised;
  - what else is important?;
  - what are the interactions?;
  - when are they most important (now, later).

169

- Interface to customers, markets, competition (this is often the section where most new thinking arises in groups):
  - issues already raised;
  - what else is important?;
  - what are the interactions?;
  - when are they most important (now, later)?;
  - changes in barriers to entry or exit;
  - new players.

- Internal factors:
  - issues already raised;
  - what else is important?;
  - what are the interactions?;
  - when are they most important (now, later)?;
  - part of organization to follow up.

Use memorable quotes from the interviews to enliven the issues workshops, and, at the end of the issues workshops, any options for strategy that have emerged should be captured for evaluation.

SCENARIO-CREATION WORKSHOPS

The agenda in Table III.5.1 works well for management teams. For disparate groups, who do not share assumptions, a longer timescale may be required. Global Business Network organize scenario workshops that take a week. It is best if the workshop is residential, to allow extra discussion time: at the very least, it must be off-site.

The scenario workshop should involve the whole team and be limited to the team. After the workshop, the scenarios should be written up by one person, who also identifies trigger or branch points between scenarios. In writing scenarios, speculation and evidence-based elements need to be distinguished.

Table III.5.1	**Agenda for a two-day workshop**

Day 1:

a.m.: meet, introductions

- questions for the Oracle
- review process to be followed (see Section III.2)
- brainstorm factors

p.m.:

- separate out the likely givens from the trends and uncertainties (see Section III.6); mapping all the issues captured to date on a predictability/uncertainty vs. importance matrix
- cluster the uncertainties into building blocks – maybe four or five
- decide on the interesting combinations; choose from two to four as scenarios

Day 2:

a.m.:

- review the combinations
- write a scenario story for each chosen combination

p.m.:

- describe an evolution sequence for each
- look for turning points
- review Oracle questions
- discuss the implications.

WORKSHOPS BASED ON EXISTING SCENARIOS

Working with business units and basing the workshop on existing scenarios (as in Section I.8) allows the team to:

- familiarize themselves with scenario thinking;

- work with views of the future;

- extend the scenarios to describe the impact on their own business;

- develop a set of plans based on the scenarios.

An agenda is given in Table III.5.2.

Table III.5.2 *Agenda for a one-day workshop*	
Aim:	Develop strategy for organization
	• Envisage the futures
	• Brainstorm the changes
	• Plan development programme
Attendees:	Functional group, management team, planning team
Pre-reading:	Scenarios
Duration:	$2 \times \frac{1}{2}$ days or one day
First module:	• Briefing on scenarios
	• Brainstorm: events and trends specific to the business or function
	• Build list of services for 2005 (syndicates for each scenario)
	• Report back
Second module:	• Assess for each service or market: effect of trends and scenarios, size of market, key skills, core/ bought in
	• Report back from syndicates
	• Five top opportunities
	• Report back
	• Action planning

TOOLS FOR USE IN WORKSHOPS

Using tools can significantly improve the results of planning events or activities by:

- increasing the number of ideas generated;

- increasing communication between individuals and groups;

- increasing the clarity of common understanding;

- increasing the resilience and coherence of the scenarios.

There is a good discussion in Azim (2000).

Traditionally, flip charts and overhead foils have been used: even the simple step of replacing these with capture on word-processed documents, which can be communicated using email, often carries significant dividends.

During the building of scenarios, tools come in at several stages:

- generating ideas;

- capturing ideas and finding common content;

- grouping the ideas and factors into themes;

- sorting the ideas and factors into trends and uncertainties;

- testing the logic with influence diagrams.

Generating ideas

With groups that have not been exposed to scenario thinking before, it can increase the comfort factor if a groupware tool is used to generate and display ideas. One such tool is Ventana, details on http://www.ventana.com

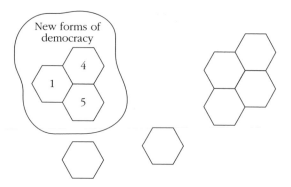

Figure III.5.1   Clustering group systems software.

Capturing ideas and finding common content
Tools can reduce the time needed to analyse interview data. One which is used by the sizeable research group at the University of St Andrews is the NUD*IST software package. Details are on http://www.qsr.com.au

Grouping the ideas
One widely used method of grouping ideas (Figure III.5.1) uses IDON's hexagons. These are about six inches across, and can be written on with felt tip pens and wiped clean to make changes. Each member of the group contributes as many ideas and factors on hexagons (one per hexagon). These are then grouped with discussion into similar ideas or themes, which will form the building blocks of the scenarios (Galt et al., 1997). IDON (now trading as Metabridge) also provide software to aid in the documentation of workshop discussions and outputs. More detail can be found on http://www.idongroup.com

Sorting into trends and uncertainties
The standard tool used to sort ideas and factors is the two-dimensional matrix shown in Figure III.5.2. Group discussion in workshop mode is an essential aspect of this step. It develops a consensus on the trends – the forces or changes which are relatively well expected – and the uncertainties.

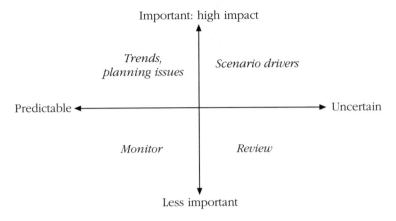

Figure III.5.2 Trends and uncertainties.

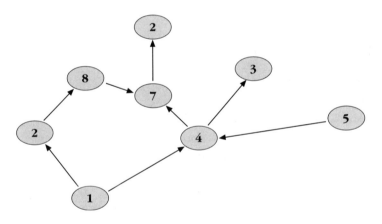

Figure III.5.3 Influencing diagram.

Influence diagrams

These are important for identifying the driving forces and testing the logic of the scenarios (an example is shown in Figure III.5.3). A tool that allows a group cooperatively to create a logic flow system is Decision Explorer: details can be found on http://www.banxia.com

Scenario creation

This section describes building a basic set of scenarios, and ensuring that they are believable and coherent. Creation of story-lines and characters take different skills from the analysis stage of scenario building. It is also important to decide how many scenarios are needed and the relative importance of external and internal factors.

STRUCTURING THE IDEAS

This is one of the most important steps in creating a common vocabulary and understanding, and is done with a nominated group of people. External consultants are nearly always used for this step in both public policy and public sector work. One of the tools for structuring ideas is an influence diagram, which shows what contributes causally to what factor. An example, using the development of violence and social unrest, is shown in Figure III.6.1 (from van der Heijden, 1996). Other groups use the hexagons discussed in "Interviews and workshops" (Section III.5).

TYPES OF SCENARIO

How scenarios are used in strategic planning and management depends on the organization's possibility of influencing the occurrences described in the scenarios. Alexander Fink from ScMI distinguishes three different types of scenario.

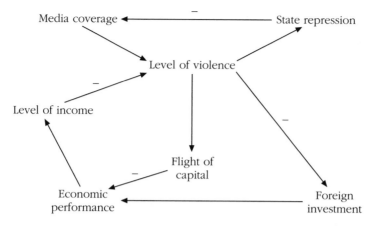

Figure III.6.1 Starting an Influence Diagram (published by permission of John Wiley & Sons, Ltd: van der Heijden, 1996).

External scenarios

External scenarios exclusively consist of external influences that cannot be controlled by the organization. A city government, for example, must take account of increased mobility and choices available to people, and of technological advances.

Internal scenarios

Internal scenarios exclusively take factors under the organization's control into account; for example, in the case of Consignia, they are free to develop new products within the scope defined by the regulator.

System scenarios

System scenarios are a mixed form of external and internal scenarios. Here the scenario field contains external environmental influences as well as internal guidance dimensions. In this case, the scenario field presents the complete system of decision field and environment. System scenarios have to be handled with special care because they contain environmental conditions as well as action options. Most public policy and public sector scenarios need to include internal and external factors.

BUILDING THE SCENARIOS

The first step is sorting into trends and uncertainties, usually, as in Figure III.5.2, on a whiteboard at a scenario workshop. Discussion among workshop members is crucial at this stage, and the matrix provides the context for this.

The trends are pulled out as common to all scenarios (e.g. demographic trends). The important uncertainties are grouped, using Post-it notes, hexagons or influence diagrams, until a few – up to four are manageable – big ideas are visible and agreed on, and posed as a question (e.g. will society be individualistically inclined or communitaire?).

Then a matrix is developed, with the big ideas along the top, and values shown as "yes" or "no". Each combination is given a name, and the interesting combinations to be followed up as scenarios – by developing a storyline – are agreed. Part of the matrix for the leading and trailing scenarios in Section I.5 is shown in Table III.6.1.

Table III.6.1 Trailing and leading scenarios			
	Integrate entrepreneurship, education and financial system	*Education, especially using IT*	*New regulatory regime*
Leading	Yes	Yes	Yes
	Yes	Yes	No
	Yes	No	Yes
	Yes	No	No
etc.			
Trailing	No	No	No

In this case, the scenarios were chosen to be very coherent to simplify their adoption.

HOW MANY SCENARIOS? AND WHAT TYPES?

Four/three/two? More?

Generally, more than four is too many for the differences to be clear and useful – but there are exceptions. The list below identifies strategies for choosing the number and type of scenario and looks at target audiences:

- Four scenarios encourage divergent thinking and are useful for creating vision:

  o difficult to maintain clarity of separation;

  o often the consequence of two-dimensional thinking (e.g. orthogonal axes and population of each quadrant);

  o one quadrant often not viable, though it may be the desired world for a business;

  o four scenarios may be chosen to represent "visionary", "business as usual", a difficult scenario and a benign environment.

- Three scenarios lead to the expectation that one is "the forecast":

  o in engineering-led organizations, often a belief that "the middle one" is the best estimate;

  o based on high/low growth interpretation of scenarios;

  o not so applicable when scenarios are qualitatively different.

- Two scenarios allow two very distinct (not necessarily "low" or "bad" vs. "good" or "high") scenarios to be developed:

  o comparatively easy to communicate;

  o best for mass use in building common language;

179

○ one version may be "official future" or default scenario vs. visionary scenario.

● It may be that the data used to create future worlds give natural groupings that lead to a specific number of scenarios. All of these can be used to consider options for action, though they may be grouped later (Section I.3, "Mission and consequences in Bueren").

● If there are several competing technologies, each may define a different scenario for "how the world might be", and then there would be as many scenarios as technologies, as in the case study of the manufacturing company KRONE in Ringland (1997).

● Consider choosing scenarios including one "surprise-free" scenario based on existing trends, an "ideal" future for the organization (normative scenario) or worst-case fears about the future.

Target audience

● Experts developing new strategies:

○ as many scenarios as fit the main competing underlying technologies, policies or geographies;

○ each technology, policy or geography is treated as a different world;

○ normally, the number of scenarios gets reduced after preliminary analysis.

● Planners:

○ two if detailed modelling of each scenario is planned;

○ four if trying to explore a new competitive environment, major changes in culture, etc.;

○ often professionally interested in exploring underlying assumptions and connections.

- Senior decision makers:

  - two scenarios to ensure that the two-minute synopsis (the elevator speech) can capture the essence of the difference between the two worlds;

  - possibly three if a workshop is planned to examine the implications of the scenarios for strategy;

  - four are usually lethal;

  - mostly interested in early indicators or predictors and what to do next about a specific current issue.

- Middle managers and business unit managers:

  - as for senior decision makers.

- Mass communication:

  - two for clarity;

  - four if all four are equally of interest;

  - all scenarios communicated must be compelling and different visually and qualitatively.

DEVELOPING THE STORYLINE

The storyline that expresses the scenario needs to communicate the important aspects of the scenario, being in addition provocative, memorable and vivid. At the same time:

- A story needs to have a beginning (maybe in the past), a middle (maybe the near future) and an end (e.g. at the end of the scenario timescale).

- The story needs to be anchored in the past and leading to hypothetical events in the future. Using prototypical characters is often helpful: What sort of people would dominate in each scenario and which lose out?

- The logic of each scenario needs to be capturable in a simple diagram, allowing it to be understood as a whole. This underpins "the elevator speech" which is the two-minute description covering all the scenarios.

- The differences between the scenarios should be clear, and names are an important part of aligning them to different worlds.

- Internal consistency is improved by using influence diagrams to see the causal connections between events.

- A sequence of events should populate the storyline in time sequence, expressed in terms that relate to observables (e.g. "UK joins the European common currency", not "UK pulls closer to Europe").

- A small set of elements are defined for all the scenarios, and their different values or outcomes are described for each (e.g. in one scenario "Schools have metal detectors and armed guards and are locked up out of school hours" and in another "Schools are used by all the community for 14 hours per day").

- Key variables should be quantified and early indicators listed. Early indicators should be events or variables tracked by the organization, unless they are very short term, and can be checked by a specific piece of research.

STORYLINES FOR SPECIAL PURPOSES

- In organizations that are not experienced in scenario thinking, it can be helpful to write a "surprise-free" scenario, representing the official future of the organization. This may flesh out the fact that different parts of the organization are operating under different assumptions.

- Phantom scenarios can be developed to explore the logical outcomes of particular sets of assumptions held in the organization, as a way of testing their validity.

- Peter Schwartz (1992) describes some of the considerations in composing a plot for a scenario. The time line needs to be clear – as do cause and effect. The characters should be believable and differentiated. The story needs a beginning, middle and an end point (e.g. scenarios for Scotland in 2010).

- Three principles have been applied to the "Foresight Futures 2001" scenarios: symmetry, balance and triangulation.
  - symmetry is equivalent effort devoted to the elaboration of all the scenarios chosen;
  - balance is scenario storylines and indicators developed as neutrally and dispassionately as possible – covering the same domains and seeking to avoid bias towards or against any particular scenario;
  - triangulation is a process of ensuring that the distinctiveness and coherence of scenarios is retained (mainly by viewing the narratives side by side).

TAKING ACCOUNT OF MAJOR SHOCKS

The approach used in scenarios might suggest that change occurs gradually along a single trajectory. Future states are seen as being the outcome of an accumulation of changes over time that all point in the same direction. But not all change is like this. The direction of change may itself vary over time, with one set of conditions being replaced by a new set. This change in direction may take place slowly (as part of the process of economic and social development), or it may happen suddenly as a result of major, surprise external events (such as terrorist attacks or rapid changes in the natural environment). If the change is slow it may be possible for one scenario to be superseded by another (a shift from *world markets* to *global responsibility*, as in Section I.8, Foresight Futures 2001). If the change is sudden, the question to be asked is how "resilient" a given scenario is to its impact. Answering this question will be very difficult, mainly because large-scale, unanticipated events are hard to foresee. Berkhout (2001) suggests that governments and other organizations build up inventories of "shock" events, by scanning conventional and unconventional sources and through brainstorming. The question of resilience could then be investigated by applying the shock to each of the scenarios and trying to assess how easily each of them could recover or adapt to their impacts.

Scenarios to plans

This section discusses making decisions about what to do based on scenarios, and provides a set of matrixes to help the analysis and decision process depending on the risk profile of the organization. It is based on the methodology used by ScMI as described by Dr Alexander Fink, and is reproduced by permission of ScMI.

INTRODUCTION

One of the ways in which scenarios are used is to support decision processes in strategic planning.

On the one hand, this can relate to the evaluation of alternatives. This could be, for example, in regard to proposed capital projects or competing product development projects, or the evaluation of existing strategies or strategy variants. The evaluation of pre-existing decisions and strategies is a *passive scenario transfer* (i.e. one or more of the action options that are examined with the help of scenarios already exist). In this case, opportunities and risks related to every aspect within the individual scenarios have to be considered. The scenarios become "testing environments" for strategies and decisions. On the other hand, scenarios can be used for the creation of new strategies at any level in the organization and across functional areas. The updating and creation of strategies is an *active scenario transfer*. The stages of scenario-supported strategic planning are shown in Figure III.7.1. This section concentrates on Stage 3 of this process, "Strategy finding", and on 4(c), "Strategic positions".

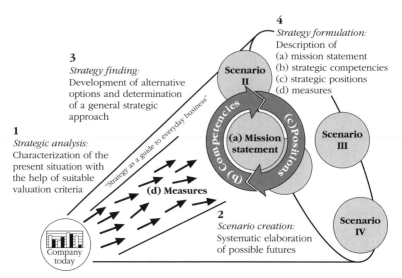

Figure III.7.1 The four stages of strategy (reproduced by permission of ScMI).

STRATEGIC ANALYSIS

Strategic analysis is the first step. It describes the current situation with the help of suitable methods and tools – using well-known instruments of strategic planning like portfolio analysis, critical success factors, PIMS or SWOT analysis, or business segmentation.

SCENARIO CREATION

The second stage, *scenario creation*, describes possible future developments affecting the organization. By proceeding systematically, even decision situations of high complexity and uncertainty can be included and made manageable for the next step.

STRATEGY FINDING

The central step in creating new plans is *strategy finding*. First, review the opportunities, threats and their related options for action that have been determined in the different scenarios. Here, the rule of thumb is to keep all scenarios "in the game for as long as possible". This way the opportunities and (often suppressed) risks of a superficially viewed "good" development, occurring in a mostly negative scenario, can be determined. Similarly, there may be a mixture of opportunities and threats in scenarios that are regarded as positive. At the end, planners and managers of the scenario project have to decide if the strategy should be built on one or on more than one of the scenarios. If the strategy is based on a selected reference scenario, it is called "strongly focused". A "future-robust plan" is based on several scenarios.

Focused planning can serve two functions: The reference scenario can be the basis of a focused strategy that presents the final result of strategy development. Alternatively, contingent strategies can be developed. These are complete strategies, which describe how an organization could act optimally if a certain scenario occurred. So the decisive question is: "What shall we do if a certain scenario comes true?" and not: "What will happen?" Afterwards, the contingent strategies are included in robust planning.

AN EXAMPLE

Figure III.7.2 shows the *strategy finding* step of a scenario project for a medium-sized manufacturer of industrial semi-finished goods (i.e. supplier to trade). Four external scenarios have been created. Specific action options have been elaborated and summed up. The scenario options matrix shows whether the determined options were only suitable for Scenario I or whether they were also valid under other scenarios. Using options that are positive under several scenarios gives a future-robust core of strategy, giving the planners the certainty: "We are relatively safe in using these measures".

Consideration of the options led to identification of a partly robust strategy for Scenarios I, II and III. These options, together with the core of strategy, now described the strategic orientation of the organization. But, because it was not possible to completely rule out Scenario IV, two further steps were necessary. First, a

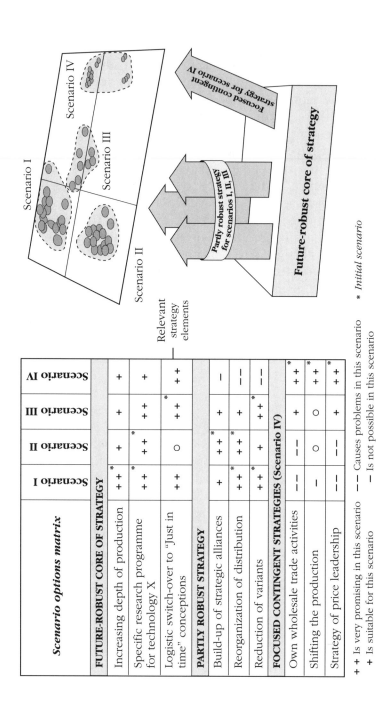

Scenario options matrix	Scenario I	Scenario II	Scenario III	Scenario IV
FUTURE-ROBUST CORE OF STRATEGY				
Increasing depth of production	+ +*	+	+	+
Specific research programme for technology X	+ +*	+ +*	+ +	+
Logistic switch-over to "Just in time" conceptions	+ +	O	+ +*	+ +
PARTLY ROBUST STRATEGY				
Build-up of strategic alliances	+	+ +*	+	–
Reorganization of distribution	+ +*	+ +*	+	– –
Reduction of variants	+ +*	+	+ +*	– –
FOCUSED CONTINGENT STRATEGIES (Scenario IV)				
Own wholesale trade activities	– –	– –	+	+ +*
Shifting the production	–	O	O	+ +*
Strategy of price leadership	– –	– –	+	+ +*

+ + Is very promising in this scenario — — Causes problems in this scenario
+ Is suitable for this scenario — Is not possible in this scenario
O Is neutral in this scenario

* Initial scenario

Figure III.72 Scenario options matrix (reproduced by permission of ScMI).

contingent strategy was elaborated for Scenario IV. Then, early indicators were identified which drew attention to tendencies of the environment towards Scenario IV. The organization has to watch these indicators closely. Should the situation develop correspondingly, the organization has the possibility rapidly and flexibly to change to the contingent strategy – "Plan B".

STRATEGY FORMULATION

The process of *strategy formulation* (Step 4) starts once the strategic orientation has been settled. Recurring parts of company and business strategies are mission statements, strategic competencies and strategic positions as well as concrete measures. The important thing about this is to see the mission statements as "big outlines that make the blood surge through the veins". A mission statement is put in concrete forms by the use of strategic competencies ("What do we have to have or be able to do in order to achieve our mission statement?") and strategic positions ("Where do we have to offer what to achieve our mission statement?"). The concrete measures finally build the bridge between the present and the objectives described in the mission statement, competencies and positions.

FIVE FORMS OF STRATEGIC POSITION

In choosing a strategic position, two factors are important. One is the ability of the organization to influence the competitive environment. The other is the organization's attitude to risk, in terms of choosing a focused or a future-robust planning style. Five typical forms of scenario-supported strategic positioning follow (Figure III.7.3).

1. React to recognizable trends
Here, the organization orients its planning around the scenario with the "highest probability". This requires the basic agreement of the persons involved about the most probable occurring future. The

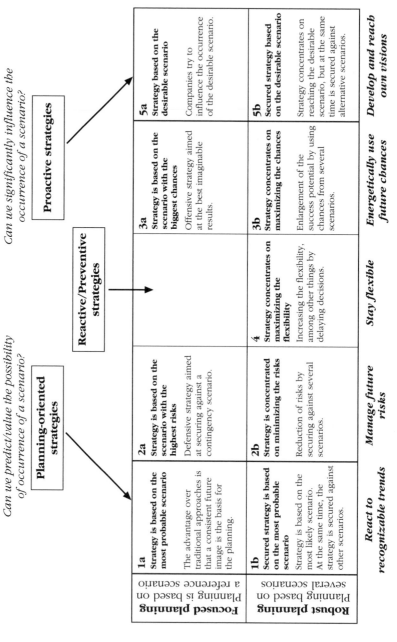

Can we predict/value the possibility of occurrence of a scenario?

Can we significantly influence the occurrence of a scenario?

		Planning-oriented strategies	Reactive/Preventive strategies	Proactive strategies
Focused planning Planning is based on a reference scenario	**1a** **Strategy is based on the most probable scenario** The advantage over traditional approaches is that a consistent future image is the basis for the planning.	**2a** **Strategy is based on the scenario with the highest risks** Defensive strategy aimed at securing against a contingency scenario.	**3a** **Strategy is based on the scenario with the biggest chances** Offensive strategy aimed at the best imaginable results.	**5a** **Strategy based on the desirable scenario** Companies try to influence the occurrence of the desirable scenario.
Robust planning Planning based on several scenarios	**1b** **Secured strategy is based on the most probable scenario** Strategy is based on the most likely scenario. At the same time, the strategy is secured against other scenarios.	**2b** **Strategy is concentrated on minimizing the risks** Reduction of risks by securing against several scenarios.	**4** **Strategy concentrates on maximizing the flexibility** Increasing the flexibility, among other things by delaying decisions.	**3b** **Strategy concentrates on maximizing the chances** Enlargement of the success potential by using chances from several scenarios.	**5b** **Secured strategy based on the desirable scenario** Strategy concentrates on reaching the desirable scenario, but at the same time is secured against alternative scenarios.
	React to recognizable trends	*Manage future risks*	*Stay flexible*	*Energetically use future chances*	*Develop and reach own visions*

Figure III.73 Strategic positioning (reproduced by permission of ScMI).

advantage of this over traditional planning is that it relies on a consistent future image that has been developed "in competition" with possible alternatives, as distinct from a default scenario often based on past experience. A focused strategy based on the most probable scenario can be supplemented by being secured against the occurrence of other, less probable scenarios. It is also possible to identify decision points in which a "transfer to another scenario" is planned.

2. Manage future risks

An organization can minimize its risk by building its strategy on the basis of the scenario that presents most threats to the organization. Specific forms of this variant are contingency strategies or contingency plans. For the development of a contingency strategy, a very extensive and coherent contingency scenario is needed, normally a system scenario including internal and external factors. An organization can also try to minimize the risks altogether by choosing a future-robust strategy based on the occurrence of all the worst threats. The problem with this approach is that it may well cause the planners to ignore opportunities. More productive is the use of threatening scenarios to actively manage the risks to the organization.

3. Energetically use future chances

An organization can build its strategy on the scenario with the biggest upside potential given by the environment. This approach is quite promising but also very risky because it ignores less promising scenarios. At the same time, it should be considered if there are possibilities to bundle several strategies into one aggressive strategy related to positive factors in the competitive environment.

4. Stay flexible

An organization becomes more flexible by gearing its strategy to several scenarios and making some specific decisions dependent on the occurrence of events or early indicators from individual scenarios. This is often combined with an operating plan based on a robust core of assumptions or factors that are common to several or even all scenarios. This combination does, however, increase the danger of putting strategically important decisions off.

5. Develop and reach own visions

An organization can also try to influence the occurrence of desirable scenarios. This kind of proactive planning mainly occurs in internal scenarios and strongly controllable system scenarios dominated by key factors that can be influenced. In this case, focused strategy development means to decide on one scenario and to use the resources of the organization following a strategy to implement it. This has two risks. If the scenario turns out to be strongly influenced by external environmental factors, it may be hard to change direction if they change. Second, an organization can become overextended if it tries to implement plans fitting several scenarios at once, while a competitor completely focuses on a single scenario that, in the end, really occurs.

A proactive approach based on a desirable scenario can be supplemented by additionally securing the strategy against other scenarios. This especially makes sense when scenarios contain significant environmental influences.

TWO COMMON ERRORS IN USING SCENARIOS

Adopting one external scenario

Organizations often develop several external scenarios at great expense. But strategic planners get discouraged at the thought of really thinking through the implications of multiple futures. Often, pressure from top managers to express planning situations in simple decision models contributes to this. So, the planners settle on one external scenario too quickly and let the success of the strategies they develop be dependent on the occurrence of this particular scenario.

Getting bogged down with alternative action options

Another mistake is made by organizations that develop and present action options in the form of internal scenarios and try to follow all of the action options at the same time. This way of proceeding violates the strategic principle of the concentration of power. In this case, competitors who just follow one direction and who consequently use their resources for the acquisition of capability to follow this direction will have an advantage.

Linking scenarios into the organization

Dissemination of scenarios is crucial for ensuring implementation of ensuing strategies. This section discusses dissemination tools and the use of business intelligence and war gaming as ways of increasing linkage. It includes ideas from an article by Kent B. Potter of Bennion-Robertson Incorporated in Atlanta, Georgia, USA (Potter, 2001), and is published with the permission of Risk Management Bulletin. For more information contact <u>kent@bennion-robertson. com</u>

INTRODUCTION

This section focuses on two aspects of linking into the organization referred to but not covered by previous sections:

- dissemination to the target audience;

- links to the intelligence gathering and analysis of the organization.

DISSEMINATION

What does a scenario look like?

Draft scenarios will be presented to the project team and various working groups to resilience-test them and explore the implications. Systems diagrams may be used to explore the

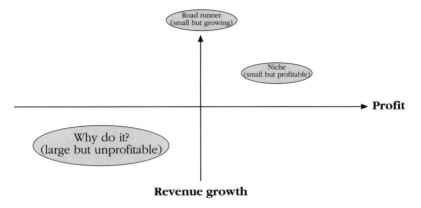

Figure III.8.1 Perceptual map.

interdependencies of factors and often provoke discussions about the underlying assumptions. However, they are probably more an analysis than a communication tool.

The most usual way of exposing scenarios back to the team or to immediate collaborators is via some sort of perceptual map. This shows the named scenarios on a 2 × 2 matrix and may give extra information (e.g. by varying the size of the bubbles representing revenue, as in Figure III.8.1).

Final scenarios

The final scenarios will need to be disseminated to several audiences:

- In tabular form, for planners expecting to rerun the current operational plan against the scenarios. But good scenarios may well not share some of the assumptions built into the plan. Many organizations believe that the best use of scenarios is before getting to this level of detail.

- To the sponsor, in slide set form plus a written report. The key slide will often be a set of recommendations.

- More widely in the organization, using a slide set plus a brochure containing illustrations and examples of the scenarios and their implications for strategy.

- Printed storyline, for wide distribution in the organization, covering, for instance:

  ○ a view of the political world in this scenario;

  ○ the economic forces;

  ○ social structures;

  ○ the role of technology;

  ○ winners and losers, heroes and role models;

  ○ early indicators of each scenario.

- Very widely in the organization, as part of discussion/decision groups (see Section II.2 and II.3):

  ○ mock newspapers, films or CD-ROMs for initiating workshops on the implications of the scenarios, for instance;

  ○ short, five to ten minutes of film;

  ○ use of representative characters (Consignia, Section II.2);

  ○ back-up data on CD-ROM adds depth (Consignia, Section II.2);

  ○ virtual reality (dti, Section II.3);

  ○ actors to play scenario vignettes are also successful.

LINKS TO INTELLIGENCE

Scenarios will live in an organization if people use them in their day-to-day work. One particularly important area is aligning the research and intelligence-gathering operation of the organization to watch emerging trends or discontinuities flagged by the scenarios. While traditional ongoing research will undoubtedly play a part, early indicators are oriented towards specific events which can be tracked through intelligence.

What distinguishes intelligence from other research?

- Intelligence is normally "entity focused", meaning that it tends to focus on named players in the marketplace, not on mass or generalized trends. This means that intelligence is well suited to help convert observations about generalized trends into clear data about specific emerging threats or opportunities.

- Intelligence is normally predictive, or future focused, although often with only the near-term future in mind.

Scenarios and Intelligence

Scenarios are most useful to the organization when they are integrated into the organization's operation; for example:

- successful at aligning leaders with a future vision for long enough to change direction;

- used to help rank-and-file employees change internal cultures to meet emerging or future external requirements;

- used to help planners who are already well connected with the changing environment.

An intelligence approach and toolkit can contribute to these aims:

- discussion about key intelligence topics picks up where scenarios dialogue leaves off, helping planners move from considerations of the future to early indicators (see Section III.2) and contingency planning (war games also offer considerable help here);

- a systematic approach to intelligence gathering aligned with the scenarios helps middle and lower echelons align themselves with the future vision by actively contributing to a future-looking, externally-oriented strategy;

- disciplined intelligence gathering as part of an ongoing system for collecting external information helps better ground each round of scenario planning.

The Thread of Intelligence

During the scenario process, intelligence has a different role at each phase (see Figure III.8.2):

1. At early stages, the organization may define broad, exploratory scenarios that identify major drivers and key trends, but not yet the entities that will operate within them. During this phase, research can contribute to the investigation of long-term trends.

2. It may be possible to identify emerging players and to flesh out scenarios within which those players have a role. This may also start to happen naturally over time. This is the juncture at which

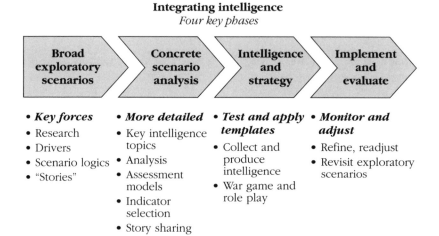

Integrating intelligence
Four key phases

Broad exploratory scenarios	Concrete scenario analysis	Intelligence and strategy	Implement and evaluate
• *Key forces* • Research • Drivers • Scenario logics • "Stories"	• *More detailed* • Key intelligence topics • Analysis • Assessment models • Indicator selection • Story sharing	• *Test and apply templates* • Collect and produce intelligence • War game and role play	• *Monitor and adjust* • Refine, readjust • Revisit exploratory scenarios

Figure III.8.2 Integrating intelligence (reproduced by permission of *Risk Management Bulletin*).

key intelligence topics should be more crisply defined and assessment models built. War gaming can also begin to be effective at this juncture, to examine different strategies.

3. As time progresses, entities that were only dimly visualized "over the horizon" during the first two steps begin to emerge more clearly. This is where more traditional intelligence collection and analysis, and fully fledged war gaming, can be very effective.

4. Strategies that emerged during the initial scenario-building processes (first two steps) and are completely defined during the third step, are fully implemented and evaluated. As part of this evaluation, planners wisely loop back to Step 1 and consider broad, exploratory scenarios to examine what "else" might be coming over the horizon in terms of emerging opportunities and threats.

This is shown schematically in Figure III.8.2.

Main points

The aim of this part has been to provide a set of checklists to help managers plan and implement successful projects using scenarios. There are cross-references to the case studies throughout the checklists, which should help recall of the origin of the checklist item or guideline.

SCENARIOS ARE PART OF STRATEGIC MANAGEMENT

Any use of scenarios must relate into the organization for:

- rationale – why scenarios are desirable;

- budget, timescale, outputs;

- framework for implementing actions based on outputs.

SCENARIO PROCESS

The process described applies to projects where the need is for:

- output for use by management to help their decision making;

- creation of vision in an organization, leading to strategic decisions;

- strengthening of a management team by creating a common language.

THE USE OF SCENARIOS RATHER THAN THEIR EXISTENCE IS THE SIGNIFICANT FACTOR

- It may be possible to use existing scenarios to achieve the goals.

- Using scenarios throughout an organization to improve decisions requires focus on dissemination tools and techniques.

- Simple scenarios may achieve as much or more than complex ones, depending on the target audience and outcome.

PART IV
SCENARIO THINKING

SUMMARY

This part provides a framework for understanding and working with scenarios, a context in which a specific project takes place, relating scenarios to strategy and to forecasting, in order to improve the resilience and utility of scenario content. It refers to the case studies in Parts I and II.

While Part III is a guide to the process and practical aspects of scenario thinking, this part focuses on content.

Section IV.1 sketches the development of strategy and strategic planning, and the relationship of scenarios to strategy. Particularly, it looks at the effect of the rise of the power of individuals on companies' strategies and use of scenarios.

Section IV.2 analyses some of the qualities of strategy and scenarios, specific to the use of scenarios for public policy and in the public sector, and differentiates between public sector scenarios intended for in-house use. Section IV.3 summarizes the main uses of scenarios today, in public policy and internally within the public sector.

Section IV.4 is cautionary, suggesting that scenarios may well overreflect the assumptions of their creators, and that these assumptions are likely to be shared by a generation or with a culture.

Section IV.5 offers guidance on technology and demographic trends that need to be considered in building scenarios and suggests that the four pillars of current Western life – work, home, education and government – are likely to be unrecognizable in 20 years' time. This section emphasizes the difference between demography and technology, where trends are clear, and the social aspects where scenarios explore the envelope of possibility.

Section IV.6 compares global scenarios originating in Europe and the USA, and Section IV.7 speculates on the major forces at work over the next decades.

Section IV.8 brings the conclusions from Part IV and of the whole book together: leading to the assertion that scenarios have a unique role as part of a broad approach to strategic thinking.

Scenarios and strategy

The section discusses the use of scenarios in strategy as organizations change their expectations and methods. As the world changes, from supplier-led to demand-led economies, the focus for scenarios has moved from scenarios in planning to scenarios in the story-telling sense. However, underlying this is the role that scenarios have in providing a forum for learning – for individuals, teams and corporations. Many strategists believe that this role is the most significant in the long term. The contributions of Adrian Davies of St Andrews Management Institute are gratefully acknowledged.

MODELS OF THE WORLD

Models of the world are often used to anticipate "real life". For instance:

- Wind tunnels are used to test car shapes for aerodynamic features. Does the car become unstable at high speeds? Does it have higher or lower drag factors than other shapes?

- Fatigue tests for airframes. Either a life-size airframe or a scaled-down airframe is subjected to stresses and strains in a test rig, where early signs of cracks, fractures or breakages can hopefully be encountered before they are seen in the airframes flying passengers.

- The use of mathematical or computer models to schedule and allocate resources, within sets of constraints. Linear programming

techniques are used to solve problems such as forest management, agricultural production, production planning in factories
and the selection of hospital menus.

It is clear from these examples that whether physical modelling is
used or whether computer modelling is used, the predictions for
real life are only as good as the ability of the model to contain
enough of the rules and constraints of real life. Two aspects of a
successful model are suggested by these examples:

- the ability to anticipate real-world behaviour – which may be
  unexpected – through exploring the constraints or changes in
  the external environment, or the relationships between forces;

- the creation of a mental model that allows the user to look for
  early confirming or disconfirming evidence.

The question for managers is how to get these aspects into strategic
thinking. It is difficult.

Clausewitz's view on how to act boldly, despite the inherent
uncertainties of war, was to suggest "an educated guess and then
gamble that the guess was correct". For a more detailed analysis,
see Herbig's article in *"Clausewitz and Modern Strategy* (Handel,
1989). It could be said that scenario planning is a set of processes
for improving the quality of educated guesses, for deciding what
the implications are and when to gamble.

SCENARIOS AND STRATEGY OVER THE DECADES

The use of scenarios in organizations has evolved in line with the
pattern of strategic thinking:

- In the 1960s, scenarios were used to provoke debates on the
  direction of society – the use of nuclear weapons, the exhaustion
  of the world's resources, the shape of US society.

- In the 1970s, scenarios were used in companies as part of

corporate planning to explore unknown environmental factors or discontinuous changes such as the oil price shock, when changes in prices changed societal behaviour.

- In the 1980s, companies blamed planning for failing to anticipate structural change such as new sources of competition. This was an era of supplier-led obsolescence, as markets saturated. Mass marketing and the growth of credit changed attitudes of consumers. Distribution was segmented and individualism (or at least niched brands) grew apace. In this environment, the approach to planning needed to change.

For instance, Michael Porter in his Competitive Advantage *went back to basics and proposed that companies consider the forces on their markets as a backdrop to planning. He considered scenarios to be important tools for understanding and so getting ahead of trends, and recommends the building of alternate scenarios as a form of sensitivity analysis.*

- In the 1990s, the Pierre Wack Intuitive Logics school, as practised by SRI and Shell, emerged as the main approach (Wack, 1985). The essence of this is to find ways of changing mindsets so that managers can anticipate futures and prepare for them. The emphasis is on creating a coherent and credible set of stories of the future as a "wind tunnel" for testing business plans or projects, prompting public debate or increasing coherence.

As the world changes, from supplier-led to demand-led economies, the focus for scenarios has moved from scenarios in planning to scenarios in the storytelling sense.

THE AGE OF INDIVIDUAL POWER

The 1990s saw the full emergence of the age of consumer power, as product quality was assured and the focus moved to service. Individualism started to change attitudes to governments and public services, assuming their role to be that of another service provider. Trust in government and institutions decreased. Deference decreased and made public sector jobs unattractive. The need for reskilling of employees and the drive towards out-sourcing are among the trends that make achieving a work/life balance very hard for the 50 per cent of the population in the public sector as well as those in the private sector. The power of special-interest groups grew and demands grew on governments. Glen Peters's *Beyond the Next Wave* captures a number of these issues (Peters, 1996), and Rolf Jensen's *The Dream Society* (Jensen, 1999) examines the new modes of consumer behaviour.

Much of this change was fuelled by globalization of the media and its scope and by the accelerating rate of technological change. In this world, it is much harder to manage public relations. It makes dealing with routine "unexpected events" such as public safety problems, medical scandals, fraud against the government, education disparities or failures, epidemics or terrorism even more necessary.

These factors are having a destabilizing effect on government, which decreases trust in politicians and civil servants at all levels. Table IV.1.1 summarizes some of the characteristics of the age of individual power.

Table IV.1.1 Changing characteristics of organizations (reproduced by permission of Adrian Davies, St Andrews Management Institute)

From	To
Command and control	Empowerment
Structured life	Unstructured life
Importance of size	Need for speed
Predictability	Uncertainty
Clarity	Ambiguity
Slow change	Rapid change and obsolescence
Reliance on processes	Reliance on people
Hierarchical or managed organizations	Alliances and coalitions
Avoiding risk	Managing risk

SCENARIOS AND STRATEGY IN THE AGE OF INDIVIDUAL POWER

The consensus of the experts is that, in this age, management is easier to talk about than to implement. Competing nostrums include:

- emergent strategy and adjustment to change through feedback (Mintzberg, 1998);

- explicit strategy as a rational competitive weapon (Hax and Majluf, 1995);

- balanced scorecards linking strategic objectives and measures to personal incentives (Kaplan and Norton, 2000);

- senior management manages values, implementation at the coal face (O'Reilly and Pfeffer, 2000);

- change and innovation by allowing employees to be entrepreneurs (Hamel, 2000);

- stakeholder model, which widens corporate responsibilities;

- passion and vision, vision and leadership (Stopford, 2001);

- etc.

How can scenarios help organizations to be successful in this age? Scenarios are widely used to:

- *explore uncertainty and prioritize issues of potential concern;*

- *pick up weak signals of emerging risks and opportunities;*

- *provide a forum for getting outside the orthodoxy of the organization;*

- *create a common language and the will to implement;*

- *focus attention on external challenges rather than internal issues;*

- *prepare for surprises.*

In addition, authors in strategic management have suggested central roles for scenario thinking; for example:

- Hax proposes that factors identified through scenarios be used as part of environmental scans. This is similar to the methods used to track early indicators, but could also be used to develop sensitive probes anticipating or starting major trends or changes.

- Hamel and Stopford both believe that organizations should use normative or visionary scenarios rather than business as usual or projective scenarios to build vision and drive their plans. This approach is followed, for instance, by the Institute for Alternative Futures in their work with the voluntary sector (see www.altfutures.com, and the case study on the US General Services Agency in Section II.1).

However, underlying all these is the role that scenarios have in providing a forum for learning – for individuals, teams and corporations. Many strategists believe that this role is the most significant in the long term.

Strategy and scenario planning in the public sector

This section summarizes some of the ways in which the internal use of scenarios in the public sector is different from the business sector and the implications for strategic work and scenarios. Section II.5 contains a view from a practitioner of some of the obstacles to effective use of scenarios in the public sector.

THE PUBLIC SECTOR

What are the characteristics of the public sector? Why should strategic planning take a different form here from that in the private sector?

The public sector is a major part of the economy of most developed nations, and the voluntary sector an increasingly important part. The role of parts of the public sector is different from that of the private sector, though many services provided by the private sector in North America are provided, or have been provided, through the public sector in Europe (e.g. large parts of health care, of transport, of telecommunications). In spite of this, comparatively little attention has been given until recently to strategy for the public and voluntary sectors compared with that for business.

Since it appears to be culturally, rather than economically, determined whether many services are supplied by the private or not-for-profit sectors, it may be that the significant factor is not who owns the services – in the sense of shareholding – but who controls them: Is the organization subject to individual consumer needs and wants or is it directed by the state or dominant monopolies?

211

When we take this set of questions, we find that there are two very different types of private sector organization:

- Those such as retailers and financial services companies, which deal direct with the public, and manufacturing companies such as food, automotive and pharmaceutical companies, which are driven by consumer choice through intermediaries, albeit with a strong regulatory regime in some industries.

- Those dominated by government either as a regulator or sole purchaser such as telecommunications companies and other utilities, or defence companies. While many utilities have now been privatized and opened up to competition and consumer choice over the past decades, much of the organizational behaviour is still reminiscent of state monopolies

Similarly, among organizations owned by government or not-for-profits, two types appear:

- central government and local government, where consumers individually have no voice, except by moving house or business location (government owns and government controls) – see for example Section I.3 on Bueren; and

- a sector containing schools and universities, health services, airlines, postal services, religious foundations, where ownership in different countries may be public, private or not-for profit, and consumer expectation and choice determines the viability of the organization.

In the *government owns and government controls* sector, revenues may be partly from consumers or business (as in local government), but government funding forms a major share of income. In the *government/not-for-profit* sector that is subject to consumer choice, organizations have income as well as outgoings, and hence in this sense operate under somewhat similar rules to private sector organizations.

However, a complicating factor in the public sector subject to

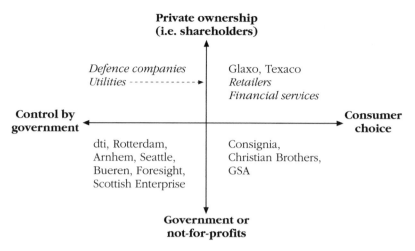

Figure IV.2.1   Who owns and who controls?

consumer choice is the need often to meet government as well as customer expectations. For instance, in education, funding in the UK is often of two categories: grants – related to the planned number of students – and fees – directly collected from students. And in some countries, health services in the public sector do not allow choice of doctor, in others they do.

Finally, organizations subject to consumer choice may migrate between the government/not-for-profit sector and the private sector, as Statoil has done recently (Ringland, 2002) and telecommunications did across Europe as part of liberalization in the 1990s.

Figure IV.2.1 summarizes the discussion by showing some of the organizations represented by case studies in this book and the parallel book *Scenarios in Business* on an "own/control" matrix. I am indebted to Sue Roberts of the Open University for starting this train of analysis and to Dr Gordon Ringland for powerful insights.

STRATEGY

A recent flurry of books and articles have studied aspects of strategy in the public sector; for instance:

- Scholes and Johnson (2000) extends a series on corporate strategy to a volume on public sector strategy, based on US experience and nomenclature, but including a chapter on global influences on the public sector.

- One important purpose of government is the management of risk. These may arise from the physical or economic environment, changes in public perception or needs, changes in technology or in political changes (Fone and Young, 2000).

- Paul Joyce identifies some of the key issues for public sector managers as governance, involving the public, transformation strategies, managing crisis and interorganizational planning (Joyce, 1999).

- Strategic management in non-profit organizations is treated by Hay (1990), with emphasis on techniques and measures for evaluating objectives, strategies and policies.

- The higher education sector is the subject of Watson (2000), who concentrates on how education establishments have to adapt to meet the needs of its rapidly changing host society as well as those of its internal community while keeping historical commitments.

- The focus in the public sector on better services and products at lower cost in (Oman et al., 1992) highlights a crucial difference between the public and private sectors: typically, the public sector has not seen its role as providing a better service at a higher cost to those who want to afford it, unlike an option in the private sector.

- Michael Porter's work on the new agenda for the voluntary sector – creating value – carries his strategic thinking forward to this domain (Porter, 1999).

SCENARIO PLANNING IN THE PUBLIC AND VOLUNTARY SECTORS

The government-owned and -controlled sector has been the environment for most public policy scenarios (as in Part I). The exception is the NGO, the World Business Council for Sustainable Development, which has facilitated the development of scenarios to present choices to companies and governments (Section I.6).

The case studies in Part II are examples of the use of scenarios in developing strategy in organizations, and of their use in opening up new horizons for strategic change. How do these differ from scenario projects for private sector organizations? How have scenarios been used as internal management tools rather than as part of an external consultation process?

In some ways, public and private sector organizations are very similar, for instance, the US General Services Agency is facing the challenge of e-commerce like many private sector organizations, Consignia is concerned to develop new products to meet new competition, the Christian Brothers are seeking to compete against other educational institutions, the dti was examining its role as government restructured. And the New Jersey Transportation Plan scenario project had a timescale of 25 years, similar to timescales used in the oil and utility industries (Bonnett and Olson, 1997).

The differences seem to lie in a number of aspects; for example:

- the stated need to bring staff alongside, much more in evidence than in the private sector, and hence the need to find a communication tool to open up the scenarios for staff;

- use of a "vision" component or visionary scenario to articulate the future;

- the predominance of external consultants in scenario projects in the public sector;

- the longer timescale of projects in the public sector, reflecting the need for wider consultation internally and externally;

- additionally, Tom Ling in Section II.5 suggests that the way in which scenarios and future thinking contributes to policy creation in the UK is opaque.

Finally, Matzdorf and Ramage (2000) comment that scenario workshops in the public sector often involve "managers who did not consider themselves very creative or imaginative, nor did they think that creativity was part of their job." She finds that short taster workshops (from half a day to two days) can be very successful in creating wide-ranging scenarios, but emphasizes the necessary pre-work and writing up of the scenarios after the event. She agrees with Annette Hutchinson, who found that she needed to define an official future encompassing at least technological and demographic changes before she could engage the staff at Consignia (Section II.2).

Where are we now?

This section identifies ways in which scenario thinking is being used in public policy and internally in public sector and voluntary organizations. The challenges of political and economic uncertainty, restructuring across boundaries, plus the complexities of the decision-making process place high demands on scenarios.

SCENARIOS IN PUBLIC POLICY

Since the early use of scenarios in the 1960s to engage public opinion, scenarios have been used extensively to engage the public through creating coherent visions of the future.

In the list below, an asterisk (*) indicates a case study taken from Scenario Planning – Managing for the Future (Ringland, 1997).

Scenarios for countries
- Scenarios for countries were used to create a common vision and agree an implementation plan in Norway's "Scenarier 2000" in 1987 (Hompland and Hompland, 1987).

- In Canada, scenarios have been used in a project involving private sector organizations and government to create a shared view of "how to organize ourselves and govern ourselves in a world of rapid change and increasing interconnection" (Rosell, 1995).

- Adam Kahane's work in South Africa has led to subsequent studies in Guatemala and Columbia (Kahane, 2000).

- In Scotland, scenarios have been used to develop a public vision of desirable futures with "The High Road" and "The Low Road" (McKiernan et al., 2000, see Section I.4).

- Insurance company Erste Allgemeine Versicherung anticipated the fall of the Berlin Wall and the consequent changes in Central Europe and so made early plans to expand in Central Europe.*

- United Distillers (now United Distillers and Vintners) has carried out a number of scenario development exercises to assess the future of markets such as India, South Africa and Turkey.*

- The Singapore government have used scenarios systematically as part of their planning (see www.gov.sg for their 3T scenarios describing the tensions of the early 21st century).

Scenarios for cities and regions

Scenarios for cities and regions are being used to facilitate debate and subsequently agreement, or at least understanding, among the wider public within the area, and encouraging very specific involvement and community endeavour:

- Seattle used scenarios for the future of their city to underpin development of the education system (Section I.1);

- Bueren in Germany used scenarios to create a view of their region, as heavy manufacturing declined (Section I.3).

- Rotterdam and Arnhem used scenarios and a wide range of

engagement techniques to create shared vision of the future for their cities (Section I.2).

Scenarios for the environment

Scenarios for the environment are being created by NGOs such as the World Business Council for Sustainable Development, the EC and the UK Foresight Programme to help business and government think through their strategic responsibilities and responses. They have also been developed by companies, usually concerned to track and anticipate consumer interest:

- A scenario-thinking project at Electrolux Group developed three scenarios for Europe in relation to global warming, use of toxins, and reuse and reprocessing. Triggered by the reuse scenario, Electrolux became more aware that there was value in its products even beyond the economic use for the customers. As a supplier, the materials or parts of the product could be reused, selling the customer a service and not a product.*

- At Pacific Gas and Electricity, scenarios questioned assumptions about the "Official Future" and caused a strategy of working to reduce energy consumption. This postponed the energy crisis in California until the early 21st century.*

- The World Business Council for Sustainable Development has produced a set of global scenarios for 2050 to raise the question, for business and individuals alike, of how they want the world of the 21st century to be (Section I.6).

- The UK Government's Foresight programme has over the last decade been extending the range of thinking of UK industry and government on possibilities for the future. The framing scenarios for this were first published in 1999 and extended and updated in 2001 (Section I.8).

- VISIONS 2000 was a research project to capture and compare about 40 scenario projects in Europe relating to transport, energy, the economy, employment and other sustainability issues (Section I.7).

SCENARIOS IN STRATEGY FORMULATION

In the public sector, some issues parallel those in the private sector. For instance:

- The boundary between the public and private sector is changing, as government agencies are privatized or asked to act in a new way to meet the challenges of e-commerce or e-government. The issues in these agencies are similar to many in the private sector.

- Public sector organizations are increasingly being tasked with seeking new markets or facing new competition. This is a challenge to management who have not traditionally needed to think about these factors.

- Governments are seeing national boundaries become more porous, as they face new political and economic challenges, so that public sector organizations may compete across national boundaries.

- Many public sector organizations need the same range of portfolio and strategic management tools as private sector organizations, to deal with the range of responsibilities they are asked to assume.

The case studies in Part II which illustrate these uses of scenarios in the public sector are:

- the US General Services Agency used scenarios to rethink their strategy in an e-commerce world (Section II.1);

- Consignia used scenarios to describe customers to help plan for new services as the postal market opened up in the UK (Section II.2).

- the dti used scenarios to think about their role in a federal and devolved Europe (Section II.3);

- the Christian Brothers used scenarios to face their demographics and ability to meet their mission (Section II.4).

USING SCENARIOS

Scenario planning traditionally used possible future outcomes (scenarios) to improve the quality of decision making (planning), and the emphasis has moved in recent years from building scenarios to successfully using them. The techniques for building scenarios are well developed: the challenge is to incorporate an understanding and facility with possible futures into management thinking or the wider domain. This has led to an emphasis on:

- *Scenario planning used for team development: the process of thinking through alternative futures provides a non-threatening environment for developing an understanding of shared and differing individual and organizational assumptions.*

- *Improving the structural assumptions and data behind planning: Section III.8 discusses the role of intelligence activities in the organization in facilitating this, and Section IV.5 discusses some historic mindsets and structural assumptions which are likely to change in the next 20 years.*

- *Techniques for communication of scenarios: when scenarios were mostly used by corporate planners, a table of factors and values would be sufficient to describe a scenario (e.g. "accessible market is 20 million"). As scenarios are increasingly used to develop significantly different world views, they are increasingly described by means of stories intended to capture the imagination (e.g. Allan et al., 2002).*

- *Scenarios as tools for understanding our world today: in many scenario studies, even those ostensibly set in the future, the effect is to help recognize patterns or trends which are emerging or already relevant but had not been taken on board.*

Forecasts

This section discusses systematic cultural issues that affect forecasts of the future. It is included because the same systematics also affect the thinking of participants as scenarios are developed. Much of this section is based on "Shocks and paradigm busters" (Ringland et al., 1999) and is published by permission of Elsevier Science.

DELPHI

The Rand Corporation developed the Delphi technique, named after the ancient Greek oracle, in the 1950s as a method for gathering information about the future. It was based on asking experts in their various fields to estimate individually the probability that certain events will occur in the future. The goal was to get them to converge on future views by comparing their answers with those of other experts.

It is widely used for technology futures. This is successful because experts take a forward view of both technology in the lab and the limitations of current technology, which allows them to see several years ahead for the roll-out of new products. In Figure IV.4.1, technology forecasting is at the "certain" end of the spectrum.

Examples of the use of Delphi include the UK's Technology Foresight Programme (DTI, 1996; Georghiou, 1996), the Technology Forecast carried out in Japan for the period 1990 to 2020 (Japanese National Institute for Science and Technology Policy, 1995) and the forecasting exercise by BP to underpin their research programme (Barker and Smith, 1995). However, the

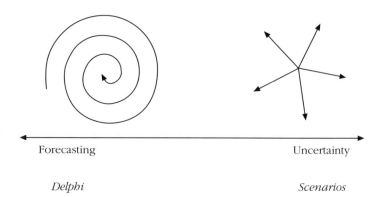

Forecasting   Uncertainty

Delphi   *Scenarios*

Figure IV.4.1   Forecasting and uncertainty (Ringland, 1997; reproduced by permission of Wiley; source: ICL).

survey of the results of the Technology Forecast Programme in Japan has shown mixed fortunes after 25 years. One strong theme was the improved quality of forecasts on a particular topic when a range of experts from neighbouring disciplines were included in the consultation process (e.g. physicists and chemists in biology foresight exercises).

In general, forecasting and trends are very useful in two areas (see, e.g., Section IV.5: "Evolutionary models for cultural change"):

- Technology developments, where technology in the lab can take a well-trodden track to the product and the timescale has a quantifiable lower bound (but see the examples of the FAX and microwave oven under "Forecasts of technological change" for rates of adoption on p. 226).

- Demography, where known birth rates and predictable death rates give predictable population sizes – though mobility and biotechnology are causing surprises even here (e.g. between two censuses at 10-year intervals the US "acquired" 40 million unexpected people). As Ged Davis says "A trend is a trend until it bends" (Davis, 1998).

On the other hand, social factors dominate the "uncertain" scenarios space in Figure IV.4.1.

FORECASTS – SYSTEMATIC ERRORS

As part of calibrating a number of scenario exercises, we needed to understand how possible it is for scenario creators to shake off the tyranny of the present, and what implicit assumptions seemed to be carried into even the most apparently radical scenarios. For instance, scenarios created by corporate employees will reflect their cultural assumptions and they will find it hard to imagine cultures different from their own. One example is the difference in thinking of hierarchical thinkers and the loosely organized networks of NGOs (Davis-Floyd, 1997).

We looked particularly at forecasts related to technology and society to see if any systematics could be found.

TECHNOLOGY AND SOCIETY

Long before scenario planning was heard of, H. G. Wells was visualizing futures based on scientific progress. The predictions of Wells in the 1890s can tell us a great deal about predictions of the future and the environment in which they are made. Wells was a commercially successful author who tailored his publications to meet the preoccupations of his readers in late Victorian England. His predictions were consciously based on gathering the trends and inventions of his present-day society and extending their development into the future. It is hardly surprising, therefore, that some of his predictions carry in retrospect an uncanny accuracy: Wells lived in a period of rapid innovation and the technology described in his novels (telephones, cars, aeroplanes) had either already been invented or was being discussed.

Other predictions, however, reveal just how contemporary Wells's predictions were. His concerns with class, the conflict between capital and labour, and the merits or dangers of government by an enlightened, rational elite place him firmly in the mindset of late Victorian social commentators and reformers. The genius and limitations of Wells were to grasp the innovations of his time and to realize that they would occupy part of the centre stage of the present. But, while his time machine remained only a device of fiction, he was unable to see the whole.

In general, science fiction and technology forecasting have a better record than forecasts about human behaviour, which remains various and often unpredictable. What has often been underestimated is the capacity of people acting as individuals or in small loose groups, relying on their own common sense. There has also been a tendency to overestimate the capacity of governments to implement.

So, for instance, similar assumptions to Wells's are visible in Herman Kahn and Anthony Weiner's (1967) *The Year 2000: A Framework for Speculation in the Next Thirty Years*. Some of the 100 things they expected to see by the year 2000 were:

- underwater cities;

- the use of the moon to replace street lights;

- the possibility of personal pagers;

- computers in business.

Kahn and Weiner reflected the assumptions of their time in over-estimating the potential of governments to implement big projects like underwater cities, and they greatly underestimated the paradigm change arising from technology change based on semiconductors and, hence, business use of computers.

FORECASTS OF TECHNOLOGICAL CHANGE

Steven Schnaars (1989) has studied an orthodoxy that he calls "the myth of rapid technological change." He notes that in the 1960s, for example, tremendous change was forecast for the way transportation would develop, including commercial passenger rockets, VTOL and supersonic planes, automatic vehicle separation on new "smart highways" and the use of nuclear power in all forms of transport.

The people who made these forecasts now seem to have been

enthusiasts enamoured of technological wonder. They went wrong because they fell in love with exotic technologies just because they were exotic. It was easy for them to believe what they wanted to believe. They also failed to pay attention to the less romantic matters of commercial fundamentals. Many of the ideas were simply too expensive to be practical. They made some wrong assumptions about human behaviour as well. Consumers might have agreed that they wanted better mass transit systems, but few were happy at the idea of sitting behind a nuclear engine in a computer-controlled bus. On the whole, they did not respond enthusiastically to CB radio, or to quadraphonic sound systems. Not all technology is wanted merely because it exists. Some ideas have come to fruition, but not very quickly:

- The FAX machine is an example of timing. Quick uptake was predicted, but initially it was too expensive and took too long to transmit a document. Eventually, 20 years behind plans, it achieved a mass market through improvements in price and performance.

- It is easy to see, now, that the microwave oven was always a good idea, but it achieved success 25 years later than expected. It was only with changes in lifestyle – women working and improvements in ready and frozen meals to gourmet status – that the ovens proved to fulfil a useful role.

Technologists work within the commonly held assumptions of their time. For example, in the 1960s, when the theme of space travel was popular, many different forecasters predicted manned bases on the moon. In the 1970s, the energy crisis became the dominant theme, and one assumption was that nuclear energy must certainly be the solution.

FOUR SYSTEMATICS

Four sources of common errors in forecasting emerge from these analyses. Checking scenarios or forecasts for sensitivity to these four may help organizations to improve the quality of the assumptions they make about the future.

The individual is unboxed

The first is that planners' assumptions about the behaviour of people, based on previous decades, are certainly not right in the current world. The basic framework of a hierarchy of needs – starting with meeting our basic needs for food, clothing and shelter, and moving on to needs for self-expression and self-actualization – should warn us that people widen the range of choices that they make once food and shelter needs are met. And since, today, most people are not prompted by memories of hunger or cold, people's behaviour becomes increasingly difficult to forecast. The common reason for failure of a number of forecasts, particularly the technology-driven ones, was that people were more sensible and capable of choice than the forecasters or planners expected.

This can cause paradigm shifts and shocks to occur overnight: not just the change of correct attitude for the wearing of baseball caps, but in very major ways such as the fall of the Berlin Wall.

Government cannot do it

The second is the major political and military paradigm shift, caused by the comparative retreat of governments. Many Western governments are trying to withdraw from the approach they took in the post-war period. Partly, it is because the ability to control their environment decreases as finance moves around the globe more easily, large movements of guest workers and immigrants continue, and technology makes the international transfer of ideas faster and more copious. At the same time, the public's demand for government services constantly increases, not diminishes. While privatization satisfies some expectations by replacing the government in supplying services, demographic and employment pressures reduce governments' abilities to fulfil their post-war roles.

In the bipolar world of the Cold War, the effort by the USA to stay ahead in technology meant that government development funding was large and assured. This resulted in a stream of spin-offs for civilian and commercial exploitation. Now that the Soviet threat has disappeared, funds for research and development have been reduced. The main drivers for technological change must now come from private enterprise. Will the sources and types of technological advancement therefore be harder to forecast?

The effect of this paradigm shift is very deep-seated: many forecasts make assumptions that the role of the government will continue to be significant.

Technology will be used if it is useful

The third source of common error is in timescales of adoption of technological innovation. Often, the nature of a development is forecast correctly, but the timing is overoptimistic. A good idea attracts enthusiasts who assume that "normal" consumers will be equally keen. Forecasting the timing of crucial developments requires an understanding of the other components that are needed to form a total system. An important lesson is that a forecast that does not materialize in the expected timescale might not be wrong in its essentials, only in its timescale; so, it should not be discarded too quickly. The other components may come from totally different fields, as in the case of the microwave oven discussed earlier.

This suggests posing the questions: Who would want one of these and what would they use it for? How much would they pay for it? The questions provide a useful counterpoint at a time of hype.

Progress

A fourth paradigm shift is a change in public attitudes. For centuries up to the turn of this century, Western intellectual thought embraced the idea of continual progress towards greater scientific certainty and a more perfect state of being. Ultimately, everything would be explained and all problems would have solutions. The experience of the 20th century has disillusioned many, and preoccupations with worries about issues such as pollution, the nuclear threat and ethnic conflict have challenged our assumptions about the nature of progress. Now, we do not think that things will necessarily get better. We think we might do well if we can merely sustain things. This loss of optimism is more marked, perhaps, in Europe than in the USA.

Evolutionary models for cultural change

Civilization as we know it has seen an enormous amount of change – social, cultural, scientific, economic, political – and the 20th century alone has seen a significant proportion of these transitions, so much so that our ways of thinking and lifestyles are transforming faster than ever. To adapt to this, we need scenarios that embrace the future instead of focusing on the past. Glen Hiemstra outlines models that can assist scenario planners in the changing world. He is founder and CEO of Futurist.com, ghiemstra@futurist.com. *This article was first published in* Scenario and Strategy Planning *in October 2001 and is published here with the permission of* Risk Management Bulletin.

SCENARIOS EXPLORE THE FUTURE

Success in scenario planning depends on being able to look at the future in the future's own terms. At the core of scenario planning is the intent to let go of the assumptions about current reality that dominate our strategic thinking. The intent is instead to open us to alternate assumptions through a rigorous, yet open-ended examination of alternative futures.

This is in contrast to many traditional approaches to strategic planning. A standard approach is to begin with current reality, and then to extrapolate trends into the future based on assumptions that there will be more of some things and less of others. For example, there will be more people and less oil in the future. Having made our predictions, we fashion strategies to respond to what we predict. But the result can often be an elegant plan for a more efficient past, rather than a truly new future.

In the new century, all planners are aware that mere extrapolation of current trends is insufficient to enable breakthrough thinking about strategy. Planners are generally aware that we live in a time of discontinuous change. As Alvin Toffler once put it:

> *Most people still seem unaware that the basic rules are changing. It means re-evaluating issues in new terms. The straight-line future runs flat into a wall.*

Good scenarios are a way of penetrating and challenging hidden assumptions, but good scenarios depend on understanding the larger context of the future. To understand this context, one must ask good questions, beginning with: "What is your image of the future?"

EXAMINING THE FUTURE: MODELS

The question is deceptively simple, and one might counter that all scenarios are an attempt to answer the question. At one level, that is true. In any particular case, however, in which scenario planners are developing a range of plausible futures, each plausible scenario will be set in a larger context of assumptions about change. Asking the image question in its largest scope is vital to establishing a plausible context for alternative scenarios. Asking the question in its largest scope is vital then to seeing the future in the future's own terms.

Where does one begin? We would argue that, despite the obvious reality of discontinuous change, there is fundamental value in looking back in order to grasp very large patterns of evolution or change. We offer two models, both of which have explanatory and predictive power to see the future.

The first model deals with the dimensionality of civilizations, in terms of the number of physical dimensions in which a civilization lives and moves (Knoke, 1996).

Dot-based culture

As we currently understand human history, from a time as long as two million years ago until as recently as 5,000 years ago, humankind lived in a world of zero dimensions. That is, they lived in "dot-based" culture. Hunter–gatherer, nomadic peoples lived in exceptionally small groups, usually only a few families. A group as large as 50 was rare. They moved about within a limited area in search of game and edible plants, but generally did not move far. Such peoples certainly were aware of three dimensions, as everything they saw had height, width and depth. But they lived in fixed dots, or zero dimensions. In fact, it is likely that they generally avoided contact with other dots, such contact being potentially dangerous. In a lifetime, one might see only a few hundred other people.

One-dimensional civilization

Dot-based civilization began to evolve about 15,000 years ago, as a warmer climate enabled farming of plants and animals. Dot-based bands began to gather in larger groups, eventually in permanent villages. By about 3,000 years ago, the transition was complete in much of the world, and nomads had become farmers and village dwellers.

More importantly, first adventurers, then merchants began to establish fixed trade routes between the permanent settlements. The "amber route" evolved in Europe, the "silk road" connected China, India and Europe. Camel caravans crossed deserts, and ships began to sail along the coastlines. Travel was one-dimensional, following fixed routes between dots.

Villages grew into great trading cities, and wealth grew in an unprecedented way. Not only goods were exchanged. Knowledge and ideas were exchanged, and learning began to flourish. Civilization had become one-dimensional, a culture of social interaction along fixed paths.

Two-dimensional civilization

Eventually, trade routes began to cross and overlap, and people began to develop a two-dimensional sense of the world. They thought about the width and length of the world, even speculating on its shape and whether the world had an end. The first two-dimensional maps of the world were drawn. A concept of society emerged in which people in villages in every direction were considered part of the whole. Leaders of great trading centres saw an opportunity to accumulate wealth and power by using the roads to grab control of vast territories, and empires were born.

Shipping expanded, and then ushered in the full transition to a two-dimensional culture in about the 15th century. Shipbuilders discovered how to build large ships seaworthy enough and with technology that enabled them to sail close to the wind and out of sight of land. The "age of discovery" that resulted wrote the concluding chapter of civilization's shift to two dimensions. Within a short 35-year span, European ships rounded the Horn of Africa, reached the Americas, and sailed around the world.

This new power in two dimensions led within five centuries to a world in which 25 nations in Europe held a tight grip on 84 per cent of the world's land mass. Evolution into two dimensions was complete, and humankind was in an era of free travel over the earth's surface.

Three-dimensional civilization
Even as the two-dimensional world reached completion, adventurers began to experiment with movement in the third dimension. For two centuries, people attempted to fly using primitive balloons and gliders. Then, just one thousand days into the twentieth century, powered flight became a reality. Within a dozen years, aeroplanes were being used in warfare. Passenger service followed soon after. By 1950, 20 million people took commercial flights, and, by 2000, over a billion were flying each year. Rockets launched people and satellites into the more distant third dimension. The emergence of three-dimensional culture again spawned new social and political orders, and humanity even began to conceive of the earth itself as a spaceship travelling in three dimensions.

Comparing the civilizations
Understanding the common themes within this framework gives an enhanced ability to see the future. One-dimensional civilization

lasted about 5,000 years, beginning with recorded civilization. Two-dimensional civilization lasted about 500 years, culminating with the great conquest of the seas. Three-dimensional civilization has lasted about a century, and has been dominant for about 50 years. So change accelerates.

In addition, cultures do not move in lock step together along this evolutionary path. Even today, there are peoples effectively living in one dimension, others in two and others in three. Each new dimension increases the degree of freedom and action, and generates unpredictable new opportunities; wealth, learning and power accumulate to those who move into the higher dimension.

Finally, in each shift of dimensions, it would have appeared at the outset that the suppliers of the tools of new dimension would become the wealth leaders. But it is not so. Rather, it is the users of the tools of the new dimension that eventually emerge as the new wealth leaders. Thus, it was not the carpenters and ship-builders of the age of discovery that became the wealthiest, but rather the users of these ships. Likewise, the suppliers of oil to three-dimensional civilization become wealthy indeed, but it is the users of this tool who generate the greatest wealth and opportunity.

Four-dimensional civilization

Now, we have begun the move into a fourth dimension, the dimension of cyberspace. The move began decades ago, but is even now in its adolescence. The world of cyberspace provides even greater degrees of freedom and action, and will again redefine wealth, learning and power. This is a world of four dimensions, and no dimensions, a world of instant communication across any distance, and a world of no distance at all. If the shift plays out in a way similar to those that have come before, new orders of wealth, learning, information and power will once again emerge. We might also assume that this change will be accelerated.

The year 2000

Is there evidence that we have entered the fourth dimension? Few will argue with this assertion, but for those who wonder, consider the following list of developments in the year 2000, which historians will point to as evidence of the shift toward the fourth dimension:

- e-commerce became major force in business, even as the web caught its breath;

- data traffic instead of the voice became driving force in telecommunications;

- mobile phones in Japan, Nordic and Latin countries exceeded land line phones;

- optical storage technology accelerated rapidly;

- distributed computing fundamentally altered how we thought about computing;

- the working draft of human genome was finished;

- scientists produced the quantum computer and the DNA computer;

- Clay Ford forecast that fuel cells would replace internal combustion;

- advances in quantum physics became the dominant force in technological development.

The year 2025

By the year 2025, developments we now consider to be wildcards will quite likely have come to fruition, as living in four dimensions speeds up the exchange of knowledge and learning:

- We live in a data-flow culture, in which all transistors are connected to all other transistors in one vast global computer. Plugged in, we cannot imagine an unplugged world.

- Nanoscale replicators have begun to make earlier forms of manufacturing obsolete.

- Light-based and molecular computing are realities, making the limits of silicon moot.

- Genomics has moved fully beyond research and development into biogenetic treatments.

- Anti-ageing has radically extended the average lifespan.

The dimensionality of the evolution of civilization, then, provides one framework for considering the future in the future's own terms.

THE TECHNO–SOCIAL–ECONOMIC REVOLUTION

A second framework is equally compelling. It is the framework of the techno–social–economic revolution. In this way of looking at evolutionary futures, the fundamental equation revolves around technological innovations that have the capacity to change everything, and thus lead to a revolution in how we conduct our social and economic lives.

While such revolutions have happened many times historically, the last one occurred a century ago, when telephones, electricity and the automobile joined forces during the final industrial revolution. That shift is also known as the electromechanical revolution. This story, while familiar, is rarely focused on in terms of just how fast things changed for people living in industrialized regions at that time. Within about 50 years, everything changed: how we make things, how we buy and sell things, how, when and where we work, how and where we live in relation to our work, how we communicate, how and when we travel, and so on. All of these factors fundamentally changed.

The process of such a revolution can be compared with the popping of popcorn. The first kernels pop with the initial inventions. Those inventions of significance generate small industries.

Older industries begin to flatten out, a few to die. The new industries begin to interconnect and reinforce each other. More popcorn begins popping. About 30 years after the initial inventions, the new industries are sufficiently mature to emerge as the dominant ones, generating the most wealth, employing more and more people. All the popcorn begins popping at once, and everywhere you look it seems that enterprises are changing, as the social economy begins to shift. During the final 20 years or so of a period of about 50 years, an avalanche of change occurs as all the popcorn pours into the bowl.

The current techno–social–economic revolution began in 1971 when Intel sold the first silicon chip. It accelerated through the personal computer revolution, the introduction of fibre optics and mobile phones to telecommunications, the emergence of biotechnology, the development of the World Wide Web from the early Internet, the completion of the Human Genome Project and finally the creation of the first commercial nanotechnology companies. Thus, the current revolution might be seen by historians as a revolution of digital, bio and nanotechnology.

THE DIGITAL REVOLUTION

Digital technology is advancing, as we all know, by growth curves that exhibit doubling times from 18 months for computer chips, to 12 months for information storage, to 7 months for the capacity of telecommunications. There is good reason to believe that these doubling times will continue apace until 2020, when we approach human intelligence in machines that cost about US$1,000. We will awaken to find that, very quietly, we have ceased to be the brightest things on earth, by some measure of brightness.

Furthermore, these machines, and their transistors, will be completely integrated into a vast digital network – a global computer if you will – in which every transistor may communicate with every other transistor. We will be able to walk into a room, look at a very large flat screen on the wall, and say: "I would like Mount Everest," and a real-time video image of sunset on Mount Everest will become the view.

The critical question to be addressed is how to bring this tremendous bandwidth to the mind. The current technology we use, screens and keyboards, will not suffice.

BIOTECHNOLOGY

Genomics, or biotechnology, will flourish in the next 25 years. As both diagnostic and treatment techniques are perfected, we'll see longer and healthier lifespans. The most critical questions will be ones of ethics about how far we should go, and ones of equity about how shall the benefits of genomics be brought to the whole human family.

NANOTECHNOLOGY

Nanotechnology – the science of manufacturing at the molecular or atomic level – may in the end change the future most of all. Currently, our manufacturing techniques, while considered advanced, do not differ all that much from the ancient ways. We combine trillions of molecules by cooking them and then pouring the results into moulds. We might machine the final product further by scraping it. Nanotechnology holds out the promise of precisely manipulating and combining basic atoms or molecules, leading to materials that are not only extremely small, but also stronger, lighter and more flexible than anything that exists today.

Within a few years, the nanotech material known as carbon-60, or nanotubes, will be produced in quantities of tons per year, rather than the experimental amounts of 2001. Nearer to the year 2020, exponential assemblers may enable mass production with nanotechnology. If an exponential assembler is perfected, manufacturing will face a revolution as fast and thorough as that of the final industrial revolution of a century earlier.

SOCIAL AND CULTURAL CHANGES TO 2025

When we look back from the perspective of 2025 using this framework, what will be the social cultural changes we might see?

Work life
Work will have shifted from jobs to stints. Rather than work being organized around career tracks and wages and benefits, work will be increasingly organized around the short term, the project and self-managed employment.

Retirement as conceived of (and actually invented) in the 20th century will be seen as a memory. Retirement in the 20th century meant that after a period of income-generating work, a short period of elderly life would be devoted to leisure and paid for by accumulated benefits. By 2025, a reinvention of the third phase of life formerly called retirement will be complete.

Home life
Homes will have been reinvented to be more like they were for most of human history, the centre of life. Rather than the 20th century model in which homes became a place to eat a meal, sleep and store personal possessions, homes will again have become a place to do some learning, some work, some health care, some entertaining and so on.

Education
Learning will no longer be confined to schoolhouses, as it was at the beginning in the mid-nineteenth century. Rather, learning will take place both in schools and in cyberspace, as hybrid "cyber schools" become the norm.

Government
Finally, the 20th century worldwide move toward big government being the institution relied upon to tackle large social problems will have completed a shift to other institutions. The great thinker on the future, Peter Drucker, argues that growing non-profit enterprises will take on the role of dealing with large social problems.

OTHER SOURCES OF CHANGE

The two broad conceptual frameworks presented here for under-standing cultural change – first a dimensional view of civilization, and second a techno-revolutionary view – each offer a tool for knowing where we are going. Various plausible scenarios can be embedded within these frameworks, with an enhanced probability that the scenario creators can know where we are going, and thus effectively challenge their current reality-based assumptions.

They are not, however, the whole story regarding contexts for future scenarios and cultural change. Additional developments such as the rapid growth of air travel and resultant explosive growth in worldwide tourism and movement, the shift to alternate energy sources, the emergence of new automobiles with hybrid or perhaps fuel cell engines just in time to combat global warming, and mobile robots are all part of the next 25 years.

But no development matches up to the last cultural change one must account for in future scenarios. It is a development so surpris-ing, and for most people still so counter-intuitive, that it is likely to be overlooked. The development can be captured in the following image. Sometime between the years 2015 and 2020, perhaps much sooner, a global conference is going to convene to consider the question: "What shall the global community do about the impending decline in the human population?"

POPULATION DECLINE

For centuries, the human population has grown ever faster. It is an unexamined assumption for many that human population growth will outstrip the planet's ability to support the human community. It is only now being noticed that rapid population growth is coming to an end, not because of disease or catastrophe, but because of economic security, which is tightly coupled with decreases in fertility rates. Only four countries in the world have seen their birth rates increase since 1980, three of which are Scandinavian countries with birth rates still below that needed for population replacement. Whole regions of the world have fallen below birth rates necessary for even zero population growth.

Now a study has emerged that forecasts that the human population is likely to go over the top at a number much lower than previously thought: at 8.8 billion. It is even increasingly possible that the human population in 2100 will be smaller than the population of 2001 (Lutz et al., 2001).

No development that we can think of will have a more profound impact on culture than a shift to declining, not to mention ageing, populations. This future reality is imminent for much of Western Europe, Japan, China, Russia, Canada and elsewhere. The debate on how to sustain economies in the face of fewer people, and religious and national pressures to have or not have more children, will be intense. Scenario-based examination of this issue is urgent.

CONCLUSION

What is your image of the future? This is the question for scenarios. Historical perspective, evolutionary frameworks, technology developments and population trends are all concepts to account for in constructing useful scenarios. To anticipate the future in the future's terms, it is always helpful to keep in mind a final concept. As we understand the history of the universe, everything possible today was at one time impossible. If this is true, then everything impossible today may at some time in the future be possible. In the end, the future is not something that just happens to us. The future is something we do.

Comparison of global scenarios

This section briefly compares two sets of scenarios, created at about the same time, one in the USA and one in Europe. Significant differences emerge relating to optimism/pessimism and the role of government vs. the individual.

TWO GLOBAL SCENARIOS

Peter Schwartz of GBN in the USA has constructed two different scenarios, one taking an optimistic look at the future and one conveying a much more pessimistic note. The scenarios were first published in Pine (1995) and are reproduced by permission of *Planning Review.*

Drivers of change
The drivers of the optimistic scenario include the following hopeful signals:

- US productivity growth;

- pervasive new technology;

- increasing growth potential;

- increasing multilateral cooperation;

- falling global trade barriers;

- take-off of Asia;

- South American economic growth;

- improving conditions in Central Europe;

- increasing perception, response to environmental problems.

The pessimistic signals include:

- slow job growth in the USA;

- widening income gaps between rich and poor;

- rising crime and terrorism;

- mounting environmental decay;

- weak political leadership in OECD;

- mounting trade disputes;

- currency volatility;

- ethnic cleansing in Bosnia and Africa;

- anti-immigrant fever;

- politics of identity.

Descent into anarchy

The first scenario is "Descent into anarchy" (see Figure IV.6.1), in which there is conflict between the USA and Russia because of upheavals in central Asia, drug lords control large areas of the developing world, ethnic conflicts increase and the rise of terrorism in the USA. However, this is in the context of a healthy, growing global economy, although one divided into haves and

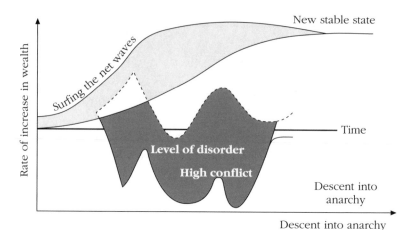

Figure IV.6.1   Two families of scenarios (reproduced by permission of John Wiley & Sons, Ltd; source: *Planning Review*).

have-nots. According to Schwartz, in this scenario, pessimism is growing not because things are getting worse but because they are getting less stable for a number of reasons:

- economic struggle and change;

- accelerating technological change;

- widening income gap;

- growth in Asia;

- collapse of Africa and Russia;

- end of Cold War restraints on conflict.

Surfing the net waves

However, he paints a more optimistic picture in "Surfing the net waves", where the sheer power and reach of technology creates many new opportunities for people everywhere. But to reach this state a number of challenges have to be met:

- joint peacekeeping efforts in Central Asia and the Middle East driven by the United Nations Security Council;

- managing economic structural change, including making technology easier to use and hence more accessible, and an emphasis on improving education everywhere;

- low tolerance for violence and war, based on quick multilateral action;

- using the World Trade Organization effectively;

- resolving crime at its roots;

- finding ways to include Asian countries such as China and India in the first order of nations;

- discovering new methods of environmental conflict resolution, particularly in relation to China.

This scenario has been developed further in *The Long Boom* (Schwartz et al., 1999), in which he argues that the period 1980 to 2020 represents an amazing convergence of opportunities for creating a very different world.

THREE SCENARIOS FOR THE INDUSTRIALIZED WORLD

The Chatham House Forum, a foresight group of business and government representatives, was established at the UK's Royal Institute of International Affairs in 1995 as a vehicle for exploring the implications for the longer term of the complex challenges, opportunities and threats facing organizations. It operates on an annual cycle, with teams exploring chosen themes. These themes, with additional information from other sources, are woven together to create a synthesized view. Figure IV.6.2 represents the dynamics of the three scenarios created in 1996 (see p. 248).

In 1996, the Forum published *Unsettled Times* (Chatham House Forum, 1996), which described three different scenarios for the year 2015, dwelling chiefly on the concerns of the industrialized world. The scenarios were communicated through the book and through slide-set presentations.

The Forum identified a number of drivers of change and coupling forces. The industrialized world is already feeling the impact of the technology explosion, an ageing population, an overstretched welfare system and the transformation of once stable institutional structures. Economic coupling continues to occur, as marketplaces merge across borders. This makes talent and skills more widely available but also sharply increases competition. Cost-cutting and market liberalization undertaken by both companies and governments reinforce the effects of the coupling forces. The rate of commoditization in many industries is accelerating, which leads to declining profitability with adverse social impact.

Scenario 1 – Faster, Faster (FF)
This points to a world of starkly accelerating change, in which industrial transformation is rapid and innovation is ceaseless, but commoditization is even swifter and profits are never quite sufficient to cover the risk that is involved. Industry condensation proceeds quickly across the industrialized world (IW), with the population falling into three groups: those considered essential to the firm, a larger group working in affiliation with it and a substantial group who work only occasionally or not at all.

This said, a general "solution" to the issues of national governance is recognized which spreads swiftly around the IW. Social cohesion is generally maintained. The generic nature of the solution permits other nations to learn from it. The convergence of the industrializing nations upon the IW is accelerated. Nations can easily be ranked as the criteria for success are more clearly understood, and markets become even more prone to amplifying success and penalizing failure. Information technology serves as the conduit through which ever more complex work is "posted" to global marketplaces, in which the low-wage areas play an ever-expanding role. Those with the lowest skills are the most penalized.

This is a scenario which perpetually threatens to spin out of control.

Scenario 2 – The Post-Industrial Revolution (PIR)

A small shift in the balance between the rates of commoditization and economic differentiation will have a profound effect on the tone of the times. As commerce finds itself able to resist competitive erosion, it feels confident. This confidence is communicated to the rest of society. Nations are able to exploit the smooth, endless technological explosion. They can begin to offset the coupling forces that lead to commoditization.

Unlike in the first scenario, in this one relative knowledge and potential is found to occur best in physically connected, specialist networks. Detailed and protracted human interactions are needed in order to achieve success. It proves impossible to carry this out with the same degree of success across ICT systems or between remote locations. It takes the complex societies of the IW to create such centres of excellence. Nations tend these sources of distinctive competence with great care. They are given the local regulatory and institutional support that they need.

Relative economic success among the IW nations also creates the conditions for positive partnerships and thus supranational collaboration develops. The forces which dominated FF remain potent, however, and their demands have to be met. The need to coordinate a response to this, across these levels of scale, dominates the re-creation of the tools of government. Each IW nation emphasizes its distinctive competence, doing so within a common framework of knowledge-centred commerce. Societies too, change rapidly. Pluralism offers identity in a complex world.

Scenario 3 – Rough Neighbours (RN)

The third scenario is one in which FF slips off the treadmill. The nations of the IW fall into a period of general difficulty, from which they emerge in the next decade to find that Rough Neighbours have arrived on the scene. In the initial stages of this, politics responds to social stress by shifting its base, such that within the IW a rejectionist majority confront a capable minority. Adjustment processes are derailed. Joint initiatives, designed to slow the pace of change, are coordinated across the IW. A wide range of measures is attempted, none going so far as outright protectionism and all based on entirely worthy aspirations.

The effect is, however, a decade of muddled strife, from which the IW emerges fragmented and bruised, with any claim to global leadership compromised. The world is confronted by an Asian economic region, revolving around China's predominance and answering to different ethical and political imperatives from those with which the IW feels familiar. A political centre of weight has developed around a number of Islamic nations. The low-income world is cross-hatched with competing ideologies. Many of these alternative views find enthusiasts among the less capable within the IW, linked together by IT.

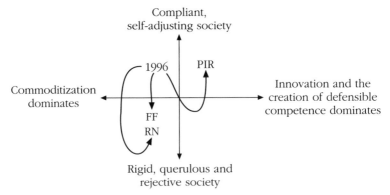

Figure IV.6.2 Scenarios for the industrialized world (reproduced by permission of John Wiley & Sons, Ltd; source: Royal Institute of International Affairs).

These scenarios are continuously updated and extended. The latest version will be found online at www.chforum.org (see Section III.1).

SOME COMPARISONS

Similarities

Both sets of scenarios flag the rate of change, the challenge of technology, demographic changes and mobility, the rise of visible unrest and ethnic tensions. Both sets of scenarios are concerned with mechanisms or lack of them to manage this change, and explore market mechanisms and world organizations in this role.

Differences

The scenarios from Peter Schwartz – and his later book (Schwartz, 1999) – paint possible visions of desirable futures and propose efforts by individuals to spread these visions and hence move to their achievement. The Chatham House Forum scenarios contain a visionary scenario, *Post Industrial Revolution* based on inter-governmental collaboration and a confident commercial sector. The European-based scenarios reflect a statist approach, while the US-based scenarios emphasize efforts of individuals.

Where next?

This section discusses some of the major fault lines facing us, and suggests that the challenges of harnessing technology will be among those needing a visionary approach. It also outlines the change in use of scenarios, from their association with corporate planning to knowledge management tools and ways of creating shared understanding.

A PERIOD OF DRAMATIC CHANGE

We are clearly in the middle of a period of dramatic change. For instance:

- See Samuel Huntington's seminal work on the change from a two-centre balance of power in the Cold War to a position in which fractures run on cultural lines, not those of national boundaries (Huntington, 1989). He particularly flagged the likelihood of population increases in Muslim countries leading to the rise of aggressive Islamic fundamentalism, terrorism and the possibility of a new Cold or even Hot War.

- Ervin Laszlo's *Vision 2020* (Laszlo, 1994) is subtitled "Re-ordering chaos for global survival" and takes as given that the changes facing us are massive. The question is: What strategies will allow us to cope?

- Watts Wacker in *The 500 Year Delta* (Taylor et al., 1997) sees convergence of a number of changes, with the power of the producers of goods decreasing and that of consumers increasing.

- John Petersen in his *Road to 2015* (Petersen, 1994) sees that information technology plus new ideas and technologies in science, plus the saturation of the planet will cause a global paradigm shift similar to that seen in the West in the 15th and 16th centuries.

- Peter Schwartz in *The Long Boom* (Schwartz et al., 1999) antici- pates three major waves of change: from the Internet, from biotechnology and from low-cost energy. The book flags the increasing differential between the USA, particularly California, and Europe/Asia/Latin America.

- Kevin Kelly in *New Rules for the New Economy* (Kelly, 1999) discusses new rules for the economy, driven by the decreasing cost of networking and decreasing transaction costs, in a globaliz- ing world where pervasive information has the effect of making the individual less constrained and increasingly aware of new opportunities and options.

- The next generation of information technology will be pervasive. Embedded devices will raise new legal, regulatory, ethical and moral issues for society. Intelligent devices will communicate with other intelligent devices. Who will police their trading? Bill Joy (www.zdnet.com) has speculated that we are already beyond the point of no return in our efforts to control our environment.

THE FUTURE OF SCENARIO THINKING

Several strands are emerging from the thinkers in scenarios. I acknowledge here discussions with Clem Bezold, Adrian Davies, Tony Hodgson, Rolf Jensen and Oliver Sparrow (Oxbrow et al., 2001) among many others, a paper by van Notten and Rotmans (2001) and the Harvard Business Review Management Update (2000).

Scenarios as knowledge-management tools

The work to create scenarios incorporates defining and assessing the most important forces and systems for the organization. So, scenarios provide a structured model or models of the world. They provide a way to organize the many action points, concerns and bullet points that managers accumulate, ranking issues in importance and in timeliness. The variables that underpin the operating environment are the likely sources of uncertainty and of competitive positioning.

If the variables can be used as axes on a matrix, then the matrix is a visual aid for the organization to discuss likely directions of change in positioning – their own and competitors. This is why the map of two independent dimensions is such a useful tool, with often a scenario moving across the map with time. The discussion of the speed and scope of change is made easier by seeing the underlying factors on the map. One example, from Ringland (1997), shows possible migration paths for the South African economy (Figure IV.7.1).

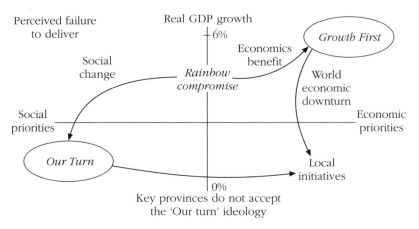

Figure IV.7.1 Migration paths for South Africa (published with permission of John Wiley & Sons, Ltd; source: United Distillers).

Once an organization has established scenarios and communicated them widely, they will start to be used as part of the vocabulary for defining paradigms – shortcuts to understand-

ing. The strategy of the organization has a context and a framework within which options can be developed. People can anticipate better what new initiatives will be welcomed and what business directions will become viable and which wither away. This is a definition of empowerment in an organization that is competent.

Short-termism and vision in a time of high uncertainty

The in-house development of complex scenarios founded on extensive new desk research does not fit with many current corporate styles and timescales. Some organizations use pre-existing scenarios as starting points for their own tailored versions for use in planning or discussion. See the discussion of "Off the shelf scenarios" in Part III.

Others concentrate on the development of visionary scenarios specific to the organization, incorporating their values and mission, to provide a framework for later work to develop implementation routes, as discussed earlier.

The presentation of these scenarios is often as a story or narrative, theatre or video (see de Geus, 1999 or Allan et al., 2002).

One technique for linking short-term decision making into scenarios is via intelligence (see "Linking scenarios into the organization" in Part III).

Scenarios as thinking tools

The process of developing scenarios is one of the few management team activities more likely to create synergy than to promote rivalry. It does this by providing:

- a shared environment for the surfacing and discussion of assumptions – most teams have members who have arrived through a variety of routes, experiences and therefore default assumptions;

- a forum for exploring the deep structure of the industry or competitive environment by thinking through the dynamics of driving forces and actions;

253

- a possibility of exploring alternative mindsets, whether in relation to future events and worlds or the current position.

GO BOLDLY . . .

A strong theme running through scenario work today is vision, or "where do you want to be?" Glen Hiemstra (see www.futurist.com) uses three keys to anticipating the future:

- Is it technologically feasible?

- Is it economically viable (when)?

- Is it socially/politically desirable?

It is likely that one of the significant applications of scenarios over the next decade is to explore answers to these questions for the range of next generation technologies.

Conclusions

Part IV has aimed to provide guidelines and pointers to help ensure that the content of scenarios is robust, by discussing structural assumptions, trends and cultural differences.

In creating scenarios for use in an organization, it is important to:

- Realize the new environment for strategy and scenarios, in which the creation of vision to allow distributed, dispersed and empowered organizations to act coherently is a key requirement.

- Relate the major axes of uncertainty to the questions facing the organization. Section IV.2 suggests outlines for the strategic questions that face many organizations.

- Understand that scenarios will build on a number of known factors likely to define the future, with uncertainties arising in the political, economic or social arenas; it is important that these "known" factors are well researched and understood. Sections IV.4 and IV.5 suggest some trends with major effects and some cautions about frequently found hurdles to forecasting the future. Section IV.6 explores cultural differences between the USA and Europe.

Section IV.7 highlights the increasing focus on the applications of scenarios outside the planning field; for instance:

- knowledge-management tools that provide a framework for understanding the current environment;

- scenarios as thinking tools to surface assumptions, explore alternative mindsets, develop a common vocabulary in a management team;

- scenarios to create vision and to explore how to achieve that vision.

CONCLUSION

Scenario planning is emerging as part of a broader set of tools that today's public sector organizations need to understand and apply. The use of scenarios for effective public consultation as part of an overall project is well established. Combining this with awareness of changes in economic and political conditions enables organizations to think about early-warning signs for identified trends, plan for possible responses of the organization and develop ways of increasing their capacity to adapt. Periodic scenario planning exercises can be helpful, but, beyond this, the organization may also seek to embed futures "routines" within many processes. Generating greater awareness about future trends throughout the organization is a condition of organizational change, and is likely to lead to a more agile and responsive organization. As Kees van der Heijden (2002) says: scenarios provide a sixth sense to managers.

References

Allan, Julie, Gerard Fairtlough and Barbara Heinzen (2002) *The Power of the Tale: Using Narratives for Organizational Success*, Wiley, ISBN 4-70842-27-X.

Azim, Tark (2000) "Scenario planning's silent partner", *Scenario and Strategy Planning*, **2**(5), December.

Barker, Derek, and David J. H. Smith (1995) "Technology Foresight Using Road Maps", *Long Range Planning*, **28**(2).

Berkhout, Frans and Julia Hertin (2001) *Foresight Futures 2001*, SPRU, for Office of Science and Technology, Department of Trade and Industry, London.

Bonnett, Thomas W. and Robert L. Olson (1997) "How scenarios enrich public policy decisions", in *Learning from the Future*, Liam Fahey and Robert M. Randall (eds), Wiley, ISBN 0-47130-352-6.

Cabinet Office (1999) *Modernising Government* (Cmnd. 4310), The Stationery Office, London.

Chatham House Forum (1996) *Unsettled Times*, The Royal Institute of International Affairs, London.

Clarke, John (2000) Governing welfare: Systems, subjects and states", *Social Policy Review*, **12**, July, ISBN 1-90339-501-1.

Dargie, Charlotte (2000) *Policy futures for UK Health: 2000 Report*, The Nuffield Trust, London.

Davis, Ged (1998) "Creating scenarios for your company's future", *Conference on Corporate Environmental, Health and Safety Excellence*, www.shell.com

Davis-Floyd, Robbie (1995–1997) "Storying corporate futures: The Shell Scenarios", *International Journal of Futures Studies*, **1**.

de Geus, Arie (1999) *The Living Company*, Nicholas Brealey, ISBN 1-85788-185-0.

Department of the Environment, Transport and the Regions (1999) *Quality of Life Counts* (Indicators for a strategy for sustainable development for the United Kingdom: A baseline assessment), DETR, London.

DTI/Office of Science and Technology (1996) *Taking Foresight to the Millennium* (URN 96/1123), DTI, London.

European Commission, Forward Studies Unit (1999) Scenarios Europe 2010 – Five Possible Futures for Europe, europa.eu.int/comm/cdp/scenario

Fink, Alexander, Oliver Schlake and Andreas Siebe (2000) "Scenario management", *Scenario and Strategy Planning*, **2**(3), August/September.

References

Fone, Martin and Peter Young (2000) *Public Sector Risk Management*, Butterworth–Heinemann, ISBN 0-75065-161-X.

Galt, Miriam et al. (1997) *IDON Scenario Thinking: How to Navigate the Uncertainties of Unknown Futures*, Idon Ltd, Pitlochry, UK, ISBN 0-95304-210-3.

Georghiou, Luke (1996) "The UK Technology Foresight Programme", *Futures*, **28**, May.

Hadridge, Philip, Tom Ling and Russell Collins (2000) "Planning to learn", *Scenario and Strategy Planning*, **2**(4), October/November.

Hamel, Gary (2000) *Leading the Revolution*, Harvard Business School Press, ISBN 1-57851-1895.

Handel, Michael I. (ed.) (1989) *Clausewitz and Modern Strategy*, Frank Cass and Company, ISBN 0-7146-4053-0.

Harvard Management Update (2000) "Scenario planning reconsidered", *Harvard Business Review*, U00009B, September.

Hax, Arnold C. and Nicholas S. Majluf (1995) *The Strategy Concept and Process*, US Imports & PHIPEs, ISBN-013458-8490.

Hay, Robert D. (1990) *Strategic Management in Non-profit Organizations*, Quorum Books, ISBN 0-89930-5512.

Hiemstra, Glen (2001) "Evolutionary models for cultural change", *Scenario and Strategy Planning*, October.

Hompland, Andreas and Redigert Hompland (1987) *Scenarier 2000*, Universitetsforlaget, ISBN 8-20018-382-3.

Huntington, Samuel P. (1989) *The Clash of Civilization and the Remaking of the World Order*, Simon & Schuster, ISBN 0-68481-164-2.

IPCC (Intergovernmental Panel on Climate Change) (2000) *Emissions Scenarios* (a special report of IPCC Working Group III), IPCC.

Japanese National Institute for Science and Technology Policy (1995) *International Conference for Technology Forecasting*, Tokyo, JNISTP, Tokyo.

Jensen, Rolf (1999) *The Dream Society*, McGraw-Hill, ISBN 0-07032-967-2.

Joyce, Paul (1999) *Strategic Management for the Public Services*, Open University Press, Milton Keynes, UK, ISBN 0-33520-047-8.

Kahane, Adam (1997) "Imagining South Africa's future", in *Learning from the Future*, Liam Fahey and Robert M. Randall (eds), Wiley, ISBN 0-471-30352-6.

Kahane, Adam (2001) "How to change the world", *Reflections*, **2**(3).

Kahn, Herman, and Anthony J. Weiner (1967) *The Year 2000: A Framework for Speculation in The Next Thirty Years*, Macmillan.

Kaplan, Robert S. and David P. Norton (2000) *The Strategy-focused Organization*, Harvard Business School Press, ISBN 1-57812-506.

Kelly, Kevin (1999) *New Rules for the New Economy: 10 Ways the Network Economy is Changing Everything*, Fourth Estate, ISBN 1-85702-8929.

Knoke, William (1996) *Bold New World: The Essential Road Map to the Twenty-First Century*, Kodansha International.

Laszlo, Ervin (1994) *Vision 2020*, Gordon and Breach, ISBN 2-88124-612-5.

Ling, Tom (1999a) "Which way to a healthier future?" *Foresight*, **1**(1).

Ling, Tom (1996b) "One year in the life of the Madingley Scenarios", *Scenario and Strategy Planning*, June.

References

Lutz, Wolfgang, Warren Sanderson and Sergei Scherbov (2001) "The end of world population growth", *Nature*, August.

Matzdorf, Fides and Magnus Ramage (2000) "Planning for many futures", *Scenario and Strategy Planning*, **2**(4), October/November.

McKiernan, Peter, Adrian Davies and Adam Scott (2000) "Scenarios for Scotland" Part I, *Scenario and Strategy Planning*, **2**(5), December.

McKiernan, Peter, Adrian Davies and Adam Scott (2001a) "Scenarios for Scotland" Part II, *Scenario and Strategy Planning*, **2**(6), February/March.

McKiernan, Peter, Adrian Davies and Adam Scott (2001b) "Scenarios for Scotland" Part III, *Scenario and Strategy Planning*, **3**(1), April/May.

Mintzberg, Henry, Bruce Ahlstrand and Joseph Lampel (1998) *Strategy Safari*, *Financial Times*/Prentice Hall, ISBN 0-13695-6777.

Moynagh, Michael and Richard Worsley (2000) *Tomorrow: Using the Future to Understand the Present*, The Tomorrow Project, King's Lynn, UK.

Office for Science and Technology (1998) *Environmental Futures*, Department of Trade and Industry, London.

O'Reilly, Charles A. and Jeffery Pfeffer (2000) *Hidden Value*, Harvard Business School Press, ISBN 0-87584-8982.

Oman, Ray C., Steve Damours, T. Arthur Smith, Andrew R. Uscher and David S. Brown (1992) *Management Analysis in Public Organizations*, Quorum Books, ISBN 0-89930-4036.

Oxbrow, Nigel, Oliver Sparrow, Franz Tessun and Patrick van der Duin (2001) "Scenario planning and knowledge management", *Scenario and Strategy Planning*, **2**(6), February/March.

Pearson, Ian (ed.) (1998) *The Atlas of the Future*, Routledge, ISBN 0-415-19697-3.

Peters, Glen (1996) *Beyond the Next Wave*, Pitman Publishing, ISBN 0-273-62417-2.

Petersen, John (1994) *The Road to 2015*, Waite Group Press.

Pine II, B. Joseph (1995) "Peter Schwartz offers two scenarios for the future", *Planning Review*, September/October.

PIU (2000a) "The future and how to think about it", www.cabinet- office.gov.uk/innovation/2000/strategic/future.shtml

PIU (2000b) "Strategic Futures Thinking: Meta-analysis of published material on drivers and trends", www.cabinet-office.gov.uk/innovation/2000/strategic/future.shtml

PIU (2001a) "Strategic Futures Thinking: Meta-analysis of published material on drivers and trends", DERA for the PIU, June, www.cabinet-office.gov.uk/innovation/2000/strategic/meta.shtml

PIU, (2001b) "Benchmarking UK Strategic Futures Work" (a report for the Performance and Innovation Unit), June, www.cabinet-office.gov.uk/innovation/2000/strategic/benchmarking.shtml

Porter, Michael (1985) *Competitive Advantage*, Free Press, New York.

Porter, Michael and Mark R. Kramer (1999) "Philanthropy's new agenda: Creating value", *Harvard Business Review*, November/December.

Potter, Kent B. (2001) "Intelligence tools for scenario planning", *Scenario and Strategy Planning*, August/September.

Ringland, Gill (1997) *Scenario Planning – Managing for the Future*, Wiley, Chichester, UK, ISBN 0-47197-790-X.

Ringland, Gill (1998) *London in 2020*, Gresham College, London.

Ringland, Gill, Martin Edwards, Les Hammond, Barbara Heinzen, Anthony Rendell, Oliver Sparrow and Elizabeth White (1999) "Shocks and paradigm busters", *Long Range Planning*, October.

Ringland, Gill (2000) "Innovation in communicating ideas about the future", *International Journal of Innovation*, March.

Ringland, Gill (2002) *Scenarios in Business*, Wiley, Chichester, UK.

Rosell, Steven (ed.) (1995) *Changing Maps*, Carleton University Press, ISBN 0-88629-264-6.

Rotmans, J., Marjolein B. A. van Asselt, Chris Anastasi, Sandra C. H. Greeuw, Joanne Mellors, Simone Peters, Dale S. Rothman and Nicole Rijkens-Klomp (2000) "Visions for a sustainable Europe", *Futures*, **32**, 809–31.

Rotmans, J., Marjolein B. A. van Asselt, Dale S. Rothman, Sandra C. H. Greenuw and C. van Bers (2001) *Visions for a Sustainable Europe* (Final report to European Commission) ICIS, Maastricht.

Sassen, Saskia (1991) *The Global City: New York, London, Tokyo*, Princeton University Press.

Schnaars, Steven P. (1989) *Megamistakes*, Macmillan, ISBN 0-02927-952-6.

Scholes, Kevin and Gerry Johnson (2000) *Exploring Public Sector Strategy*, Financial Times/Prentice Hall, ISBN 0-27364-687-7.

Schwartz, Peter (1992) "Composing a plot for your scenario", *Planning Review*, May/June.

Schwartz, Peter (1997) *The Art of the Long View*, Doubleday, ISBN 0-38526-731-2.

Schwartz, Peter, Peter Leyden and Joel Hyatt (1999) *The Long Boom*, Perseus Books, ISBN 0-73820-074-3.

Stopford, John (2001) "Should strategy makers become dream weavers?", *Harvard Business Review*, January.

Taylor, Jim and Watts Wacker (1997) *The 500-Year Delta*, Harper Business, ISBN 0-88730-838-4.

United Nations (1997) "Bruntdland Commission".

van der Heijden, Kees (1996) *Scenarios, The Art of Strategic Conversation*, Wiley, ISBN 0-47196-639-8.

van der Heijden, Kees, Ron Bradfield, George Burt, George Cairns and George Wright (2002) *The Sixth Sense: Enhancing Organizational Learning with Scenarios*, Wiley, 2002 (to be published).

van Notten, Philip and Jan Rotmans (2001) "The future of scenarios", *Scenario and Strategy Planning*, **3**(1), April/May.

Wack, Pierre (1995) "Scenarios, uncharted waters ahead", *Harvard Business Review*, September/October.

Wack, Pierre (1995) "Scenarios, shooting the rapids", *Harvard Business Review*, November/December.

Watson, David (2000) *Managing Strategy*, Open University Press, Milton Keynes, UK, ISBN 0-33520-345-0.

References

Yapp, Chris (2001) "Expecting the unexpected", *Scenario and Strategy Planning*, April/May.

Zimmern, R. and C. Cook (2000) *Genetics and Health: Policy Issues for Genetic Science and Their Implications for Health and Health Services*, The Nuffield Trust, London.

Index

Active scenario transfer 185

Boot camps 14–15
Brainspotting scenarios, *see*
   Scenarios

Case studies *see* Scenario
   case studies
Chain scenarios *see*
   Scenarios
Chatham House
   Forum 245–246
Consignia *see* Scenario case
   studies

De La Salle Christian
   Brothers 111–113
   see also Scenario case
   studies
Delphi technique 223–224
DTI 104, 221
   see also Scenario case
   studies

Economic development
   28–29
Electrolux Group 219
Employment 28–29
European Commission
   42–46
Evolutionary models
   230–231
   civilization comparisons
   233–234
   dot-based culture 232
   four-dimensional
   civilization 234
   one-dimensional
   civilization 232

three-dimensional
   civilization 233
two-dimensional
   civilization 232–233
year 2000 234–235
year 2025 235–236

Financial flexibility 23
Focal issues 146–147,
   160–166
   see also Scenario planning
Forecasts
   common errors 227–229
   systematic errors 225
   technological change
   226–227
   technology and society
   225–226
   useful areas in 224
   see also Delphi technique
Foresight Report 65–76,
   183–184, 219
   uses of 72–74
futurefocus@dti 107–110
   scenarios within 109–110
Futures planning
   biotechnology 238
   digital revolution
   237–238
   nanotechnology 238
   population decline
   240–241
   social-cultural changes up
   to the year 2025 239
   techno–social–economic
   revolution 236–237
   see also Evolutionary
   models
Futures Programme 39–40

Futures scenarios (UK) *see*
   Scenario case studies
Futurescope Group 46–47

Global Business
   Network 11–12,
   20–21, 34, 111
Global competition 23
Global scenarios *see*
   Scenarios
Governance system 67–68

Hedsor Memorandum 49
Hedsor seminar 42–43
Holland America Line
   shipping 21
Huntington, Samuel 250

ICL 104, 106–107
   see also Scenario case
   studies
   futurefocus approach 106
   relationship with DTI 104
Influence diagrams 175, 177
Information society 42–43,
   46
Information technology 17,
   23, 42
   European Commision
   vision for Europe
   42–46
Intelligence 196–199
Interviews 157, 160–165,
   167–169
   practical tips 167–169

Jensen, Rolf 208

Kelly, Kevin 251

Index

Laslo, Ervin 250
Lessons learned 77,
    132–134

Models *see* Evolutionary
    models

Newly Industrialized
    Countries (NICs) 16

Pacific Gas and electricity
    219
Passive scenario transfer
    185
Peters, Glen 208
Peterson, John 251
Pierre Wack Intuitive
    Logics 207
Porter, Michael 207
Predictable factors 47–48
Private–Public
    Partnership 29
Public policy 217–220
Public policy making 128,
    130
Public sector 211–213

Rand Corporation *see* Delphi
    technique
Research 160–165
Risk management 127–128

Scenario case studies
    Arnhem city
        development 21–22,
        218–219
    Bueren city
        development 23–30,
        218
    Consignia 94, 220–221
        futures work in 95–96
        scenario 2010 98–99
        scenario
            development 96–98
    De La Salle Christian
        Brothers 111–123
    DTI and ICL 104–110
        futurefocus@dti
        107–110
    futures scenarios (UK)
        66–76, 126–131
    environmental futures
        scenarios 75–76

Rotterdam city
    development 20–22,
    218–219
Scottish Enterprise 31–41
    developing scenario
        thinking 32–35
    scenarios for Scotland
        37–39
    scenarios with
        customers and
        partnerships 35–36
Seattle scenarios
    project 11–12, 218
US General Services
    Agency (GSA)
    83–93, 220
    enterprise model
        86–89
    Higher Value
        Enterprise Model
        86–89
    horizontal government
        model 86, 88–89
    linked stovepipe
        model 86–87, 89
    use of the scenarios
        88–92
VISIONS scenarios
    57–64, 219–220
World Business Council
    for Sustainable
    Development 51–56
Scenario creation 176–184,
    186
    accounting for major
        shocks 183–184
    building scenarios
        178–179
    developing the storyline
        181–183
    number required
        179–181
    structuring ideas 176
    see also Scenario types
Scenario planning 40,
    138–142, 145,
    153–159
    see also Futures planning
    linking to the client/
        organization
        140–141, 155–159
    development of 146, 149
    driving forces 147
    feedback 150, 158

focal issue identification
    146–147
force importance and
    uncertainty 147–148
implementation of 151
implications of scenarios
    149
indicators and signposts
    150
key forces in the local
    environment 147
planning options 151
pre-planning checklist
    153–154
public sector 211–216
publicity 151–152
scenario logics selection
    148
team members 154–155
voluntary sector 215–216
see also Interviewing and
    questionnaires,
    Research
Scenario types 176
    external scenarios 177
    internal scenarios 177
    system scenarios 177–178
Scenario workshops *see*
    Workshops
Scenarios
    adaptation of 143–144
    brainspotting
        scenarios 34
    Chain scenarios 61–62
    common errors in use
        192–193
    dissemination of data
        194–199
        in a written report 195
        in tabular form 195
        via a printed storyline
            196
        via discussion groups
            196
    for public education
        11–19
    implications and
        consequences 18–19
    global 242–249
    knowledge management
        tools 252–254
    links to intelligence
        196–198
    public policy 217–220

use of 137–138, 221–222
see also Vision for Europe,
    Scenario case studies
Schwartz, Peter 251
Scottish Council
    Foundation 36
Seattle Education
    Association 11
Social values 67
Stages in a project *see*
    Scenario planning
Stakeholders 138–141
Storyline development
    181–182
Strategy 205–210, 213–214
    analysis 186
    scenarios, and 205–210,
    220–221
    strategy formulation
    220–221
Strategic Futures Team
    32–33

see also Scenarios
Strategic position 189–192
Strategy finding 186–189
Strategy formulation 189

Team members *see* Scenario
    planning
Technology and society
    225–226
    see also Forecasts,
    Information
    technology

Uncertainties, of future
    47–48
US General Services Agency
    see Scenario case
    studies
US trade relations 14–15

Vision for Europe 44–46

Wack, Pierre *see* Pierre
    Wack Intuitive Logics
Wacker, Watts 251
Workshops 157, 160, 165,
    171–172
    Futurescope's
    consideration of
    Europe 46–49
    ICL for European
    Commission 42–43
    idea generation and
    capture 173, 175
    issues workshops
    169–170
    scenario-creation
    workshops 170–171
    tools, use of in 172
    World Business Council
    for Sustainable
    Development 51–56,
    219

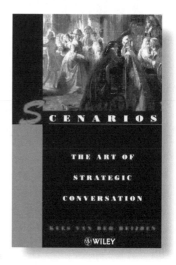